The Island Collection

New Plays By Carolyn Gage

The Island Collection

New Plays by Carolyn Gage

The Island Collection © 2019 Carolyn Gage

ISBN: 978-1-79476-757-7
All rights reserved.

Caution: Professionals and amateurs are hereby warned that *The Island Collection* is subject to a royalty. It is fully protected under the copyright laws of the United States of America, and of all countries covered by the International Copyright Union (including the Dominion of Canada and the rest of the British Commonwealth), and of all countries covered by the Pan-American Copyright Convention and the Universal Copyright Convention, and of all countries with which the United States has reciprocal copyright relations. All rights including, but not limited to, professional, amateur, recording, motion picture, recitation, lecturing, public reading, radio and television broadcasting, video or sound taping, all other forms of mechanical or electronic reproduction, such as information storage and retrieval systems and photocopying, and the rights of translation into foreign languages are expressly reserved. Particular emphasis is placed on the question of readings and all uses of this play by educational institutions, permission for which must be secured in writing from the author or the author's representative. No amateur or stock performance or reading of the play may be given without obtaining, in advance, the written permission of the Author.

All inquiries concerning professional and amateur performance rights should be addressed to the Author via her website at www.carolyngage.com.

Cover art: Emily Carr, "Scorned as Timber, Beloved of the Sky," 1935, oil on canvas, Collection of the Vancouver Art Gallery, Emily Carr Trust. Used with permission.

Cover design by Amy Jorgensen. Back cover photo by Jonathan Spath.

.

Table of Contents

Introduction

In 2016, I moved to the village of Southwest Harbor on Mount Desert Island in Maine. These are the plays I completed in the first three years of my island life.

For the cover of this collection, I chose Emily Carr's painting, "Scorned for Timber, Beloved of the Sky," because all of the plays deal with female characters who, in one way or another, have been "scorned for timber," but who have managed to find their place in the sun, as those "beloved of the sky." In fact, the very reasons for which these women have been reviled and rejected provide the keys to understanding their ability to survive and even thrive.

My work has been commercially "scorned for timber," but in my sixty-seventh year, I look around and see that I am still standing, and my plays are also still standing with me. I find myself cherishing the tranquility of my solitary perch, and it is my hope that these plays will offer a context and affirmation to others whose value has been discounted in the mainstream culture.

Black Star

I discovered Henrietta Vinton Davis in the early 1980's, when I read a chapter about her in *Shakespeare in Sable: A History of Black Shakespearean Actors* by Errol Hill. I had never seen her mentioned in any theatre history texts, and what caught my attention was her resistance to the popular culture for African American performers of her day.

Davis refused to participate in the plantation dramas, the "Tom shows," or the minstrelsy of the late 19th century. Instead, she was performing Shakespeare and offering platform recitals of African American poetry and monologues. She produced one of the first epic verse dramas by an African American author, *Dessalines* by William Edgar Easton, about the Haitian revolution. She also collaborated with John Edward Bruce in the writing of *Our Old Kentucky Home*, a startling plantation drama that ended with the formerly enslaved workers overthrowing their oppressors and occupying the estate. She commissioned plays in which the lead female would disguise herself as a male, thus enabling Davis to perform a variety of scenes in "breeches parts." She produced her own tours and managed her own companies in Chicago and in Kingston, Jamaica.

At sixty, Davis made the most radical career choice of her life. At an age when many performers retire, she quit the stage to devote the remainder of her life to UNIA, the Universal Negro Improvement Association, founded by the controversial proponent of Pan-Africanism, Marcus Garvey. She became a phenomenally successful administrator and an international organizer for Garvey's movement.

Because of her fiercely independent career, Davis was not affiliated with the Black theatres, troupes, or male impresarios of her day. For this, she has been effectively written out of Black theatre history. As a woman in the overwhelmingly male-dominated administration of UNIA, Davis's role has been underrepresented, distorted, or erased in the histories of that movement.

It was my intention to write a play that celebrated the integrity and courage that informed Davis' theatre career, as well as her vision and loyalty in her work for UNIA. I wanted to show the continuity between these two seemingly disparate career paths.

The Garvey years of Davis' career fascinated me, especially the story of the Liberian delegation, where harsh political realities collided head-on with the rhetoric-driven vision of Garvey's African Redemption. Davis never swerved from her mission or from her faith in a man that integrationist W.E.B. DuBois accused of being "the worst enemy of the Black race."

The structure of the play engages the use of flashbacks to tell the story of her theatrical past, and these self-contained vignettes reflect the conventions of the turn-of-the-century, romantic plays of Davis' day with their melodramatic arcs, heroic prose arias, and tidy endings—the mark of the "well-made play."

The scenes that frame these flashbacks, however, are contiguous and set in 1924, when Davis was in her sixties and working as an administrator and organizer for Garvey. These scenes stand out in sharp contrast to the flashback vignettes. With a dreamlike structure (dialogue with a dead man), they focus on the internal reality of the characters, reflecting the not-so-tidy conventions of modernist theatre. I chose these two contrasting dramatic styles, because the UNIA dream of

African Redemption was distinctly romantic and highly theatrical. On the other hand, the political contradictions and controversies swirling around Garvey did not lend themselves to a clear narrative arc or an easy resolution.

In today's frightening environment of escalating, overt racism on the part of government officials, I wanted to write a play about hope and about what it takes to generate and propagate that hope. I wanted to affirm the critical importance of live theatre as a vehicle for social justice, and I wanted to put a remarkable woman, largely absent from even African American theatre history, back into the spotlight.

Now... addressing the elephant in the living room: What is a white woman doing writing about Henrietta Vinton Davis?

In his essay, "How to Unlearn Everything, " author Alexander Chee, addresses the issue of cultural appropriation and asks these three questions of writers who wish to explore lives of those unlike themselves:

- Why do you want to write from this character's point of view?
- Do you read writers from this community currently?
- Why do you want to tell this story?

Fair enough. 1) I wanted to write from Davis' point of view, because the intersection of art and activism is one that engages me very personally. Davis' life has inspired me for more than three decades, and that inspiration continues to inform many of my choices. I am a playwright, and writing plays is my was of giving my attention to a subject. In the words of author Iris Murdoch, "I use the word 'attention' to express the ide of a just and loving gaze directed upon individual reality. I believe this to be the characteristic and proper mark of the active moral agent."

Beginning my career in the 1980's as an actor, I found myself unable to find roles that reflected my reality and so I became a playwright specializing in roles for gender-non-conforming lesbians. I had to not only write the plays, but produce them, perform in them, direct them, tour in them, publicize them, and self-publish them.

I have been fired, threatened, evicted, and libeled for writing and producing lesbian-themed work. My lesbian theatre company was the subject of litigation against a state arts agency, a local arts council, and a local school district. The lawsuit achieved "national priority" status with the ACLU, and, even though a settlement was eventually reached, the statewide publicity campaign launced by the ACLU generated such intense homophobia, I ended up closing my theatre and moving to another state.

I wrote lesbian-centered plays, generating lesbian archetypes and lesbian paradigms that are absent in the mainstream culture. I wanted to give lesbians a lived experience of being center stage in our lives, if only for a few hours. Was this a false hope? Was I encouraging my people to acts of self-esteem that would get them fired and evicted also? Many of the actors in my first theatre company were, indeed, fired, harassed, and evicted for working with me. All of us paid a price.

I wrote *Black Star* to explore Davis' experience with discrimination in bucking mainstream assimilation, but also to look hard at the ethics of selling an impossible dream to members of an oppressed minority. And I also wanted to honor the self-interrogation of an older woman as she wrestles with the compromises she has had to make in protecting her lifework.

2) Yes, I read writers from the African American community. I especially read biography, which is how I discovered Davis. Twenty years ago, I wrote a play about Mary Jane Richards Denman, an enslaved woman who worked as a Union spy. At that time I researched conditions of slavery and read a number of captive narratives, as well as histories of the Civil War. I have actively searched out and read contemporary lesbian and feminist African American authors: Audre Lorde, Pat Parker, Barbara Smith, Pauli Murray, Toni Cade Bambara (with whom I worked on a political protest action), Toni Morrison, Angela Davis, and Anita Cornwell. I have studied the lives and works of African American playwrights Lorrraine Hansberry, Zora Neale Hurston, Pauline Hopkins, Angelina Weld Grimké, and Ntozake Shange, Alice Childress, and Lynn Nottage. Actress Sheryl Lee Ralph, intrigued by *Black Star* and considering producing a professional reading of it, invited me to New York to meet with her backstage at *Wicked*, during her run in the show. We were in talks for over a years about the project.

I researched *Black Star* for three years, reading volumes on Garvey and DuBois, but also on the Columbian Exposition, on Frederick Douglass, Will Marion Cook, Powhatan Beaty, Sissierietta Jones, both of Garvey's wives, UNIA, African American theatre in the 18th, 19th, and early 20th centuries, the history of Liberia, and the Black Star Line. I researched many subjects that did not make their way into the play, especially the life of Poston's wife, the sculptor Augusta Savage. She deserves her own play.

3) I want to tell this story of pragmatic despair and impossible hope, because it seems to me to be important as we all look out on a ruined planet on the brink of climate chaos. Actually, that chaos has already begun in the Amazon, in parts of Africa, and in the Middle East. What is the role of the artist in this hopeless and terrifying scenario? Can theatre be relevant? Is it an act of flimflam or a cheat, as the ghost of Robert Poston asserts? Or is it our best hope for unifying and inspiring heroism, even in a doomed mission?

Finally, I assumed that, after the 1986 publication of *Shakespeare in Sable*, there would follow a plethora of scholarly biographies, theses, dissertations, articles, and websites about Henrietta Vinton Davis. Periodically I would conduct Internet searches for her name. After thirty years, I found only one website and one academic paper. The example of Davis' career in theatre, lived against the grain, had kept me going many times when I felt overwhelmed by institutionalized oppression. After three decades, I felt it was time for me to honor my debt to this brilliant and courageous artist and activist. If I have not done justice to the breadth of

Davis' life and the depth of her vision, I apologize, and I invite readers to engage with me on these critically important questions of cultural appropriation.

Easter Sunday

A friend of mine suggested that I write a play about Marty Mann, who was one of the first women in Alcoholics Anonymous, and who was also lesbian. Intrigued, I took her up on the challenge.

I began to read about Mann's life, keeping an eye out for those dramatic contradictions—the "feet of clay," if you will, that make for fascinating characters. What caught my attention was the "slip" that Marty Mann had after twenty years of sobriety, and the fact that she felt unable to reach out for help, because of her very public persona as a national spokesperson for the alcohol recovery movement.

In researching Mann's lesbian life, I read Esther Newton's book *Cherry Grove, Fire Island: Sixty Years in America's First Gay and Lesbian Town*. Mann and her girlfriend had owned a cottage in Cherry Grove since the late 1930's. I was intrigued by the rigidity of class divisions in a town where everyone was queer, and this gave me the idea of Del and Flora, as a working-class couple seeking to buy into this exclusive community.

The theme of resurrection runs through the play, from the obvious reference to Easter, to Del's recovery story and

Flora's finding her authenticity as a lesbian. The bright sunshine of Morningside Park and the gay colors of the snow cones in the first scene stand in stark contrast to the dark-as-a-tomb interior of Marty's brownstone, the site of a sordid, two-week alcoholic binge. Between these heaven-and-hell scenarios is the scene on the stoop of the brownstone, where sunlight and shadow intersect with sharp angles. Here, Flora and Del's idyllic relationship is severely challenged, and Flora abandons the quest. Del, confronting Marty as a "living dead" gatekeeper, pushes her way into a middle-class netherworld of alcoholism and class prejudice. Both Marty and Del, wrestling for dominance, descend into this nightmare world.

The play ends on a sudden grace note, when Del reaches out to call her sponsor, breaking the death-grip of her own self-will. Marty, still ensnared by pride and fear, takes a partial step toward the light of redemption.

At the time when I wrote the play, I had been an active member of Alanon for a quarter century. The play is deeply personal for me, and one of my favorites.

Lighting Martha

Lighting Martha has traveled a long way from the first draft, written in 2004. The play was originally inspired by a passage in *Staging Desire: Queer Readings of American Theatre History,* where the author described how lighting pioneer Jean Rosenthal, just weeks from dying of cancer, was brought to City Center in an ambulance and on a gurney, in order to supervise the final lighting check for Martha Graham and her dance company's thirty-fifth season.

In researching the first draft, I studied Graham's classic dances in detail, read Graham biographies, researched Rosenthal's life, studied her light plots and her book *The Magic of Light*, and met with Tony-award-winning lighting designer Beverly Emmons, who invited me to her home and took me on a tour of City Center. I discovered that Jean's life partner Marion (Miki) Kinsella was still alive, in her 80's, and living on Martha's Vineyard.

I had two phone conversations with Miki. The first one was very promising. I told Miki upfront that I was a playwright who specialized in writing about the lives of famous lesbians, and that I wanted to write a play about Jean Rosenthal, incorporating her lesbianism. When Miki expressed concerns about this, I shared information with her about how Jean's lesbianism and their partnership were already being written about in books and in articles. I told her that this project would provide her with an opportunity to help shape a narrative that was already public. Miki began to open up about networks of lesbians in her and Jean's life. She told me she had photographs that she could show me, and stories she could share. I recognized many of the names from decades of research into lesbian theatre history. We made plans for me to come visit her on the Vineyard.

Several weeks later, I called Miki again, this time to confirm the date and time of the ferry I would be taking. This conversation was so different from the first, it was as if I was speaking to a different person. This Miki was angry and suspicious. She opened by telling me that she had found my website (I had given her the URL), and that she now knew the "kind of work" I did. She appeared not to remember that I had told her about this "kind of work," nor did she remember her invitation to me. She spoke to me as if I was trying to trick her or take advantage of her somehow, dragging her and Jean's name through the mud. And then I heard the clink of ice cubes.

In my career, I encounter homophobia on a weekly basis, and it's often quite virulent. I have lost housing and jobs, and I have been involved in lawsuits because of homophobia. Miki's attack, comparatively minor in terms of material consequences, was still profoundly upsetting to me.

In the end, I did write a draft of a play about Jean Rosenthal, and it was incredibly dull. The play was structured around recreating Jean's lighting design for Martha Graham's "Errand Into the Maze." I had decided to use lighting as a second character. Moss Hart used to say that playwriting was the only profession where one could achieve a level of proficiency and success, and still turn out a project that appeared to have been executed by someone who knew nothing at all about the craft. Such was that draft of *Lighting Martha*.

I put the play away for fourteen years, even as I continued to tell the story of Miki and the ice cubes. Gradually, the pain of that conversation began to recede, and, eventually, I read that Miki had died.

In 2018, I began putting together a second collection of monologues and scenes excerpted from my work. It occurred to me that I might be able to salvage something from my long-abandoned draft of *Lighting Martha*. Working with this material again after so many years, I remembered the hundreds of hours that had gone into the researching of it. Feeling it was a shame to let all that work go to waste, I began to envision a much shorter play that incorporated my experience of Miki, designating her—instead of light!—as the second character.

One of the things that Miki had shared with me in that first conversation was that Jean had arranged for her doctors to have all their consultations with Miki. Jean did not want to know anything about the progression of her cancer or her prognosis. She had left Miki to field all of that information, and Miki was never allowed to talk to Jean about her partner's impending death. When she shared this with me, she expressed a tremendous sense of pain from lack of closure, as well as a lingering resentment.

This dynamic would become the heart of the play. I spent the summer of 2018 studying dying and writing about it in other contexts. I realized that my earlier version of Jean on the gurney was some kind of Disney fantasy. A woman, days from dying of cancer, is not going to be making energetic speeches that express complex and charged emotions. She cannot possibly take stage in any meaningful way, except as a kind of ghoulish sideshow. In my sixty-seventh year, I was getting real about dying.

The skeletal and heavily medicated Jean has left the building when this version of the play opens. The dialogue is between the angry, grieving, and overwhelmed Miki and the ghost of a younger Jean. The play is about a lesbian who was most comfortable in the shadows, throwing her meticulously designed lighting onto others—the performers. It is especially the story of lighting Martha Graham, the woman who was Jean's first inspiration and perhaps an early crush. It is the story of a life partner who feels she has had to take second place to her lover's all-absorbing career, and who is attempting to confront that before it is too late.

Jean's wisdom about stage lighting guided me in the workshopping of the new draft, which had begun as a play about grieving a lover who was inaccessible. I was directing attention on the emotional shortcomings of a brilliant artist whose life was her work. In production, this perspective appeared shallow and one-sided. I realized that the story—my play—was "poorly lit." And so I went back to what Jean had written about stage lighting. In *The Magic of Light*, she had written:

> *Before the 19th century, lighting's sole purpose was visibility. Then, it gained "theatricality," and began to be used for effects. But in this century, the role of lighting has been refined to aid communication.*

Eureka! "*Refined to aid communication!*" I had been crafting *Lighting Martha* as a kind of searchlight among the shadows of an intimate relationship, seeking out the faults of one partner in order to cast blame. No wonder it seemed so superficial! The plot was back in the 19th century, focused on visibility and theatricality. In real life, relationships—the interesting ones—are not about villains and victims. Unless train trestles and sawmills are involved, melodramas cannot hold the interest of contemporary theatre audiences.

I rewrote the play with Jean's admonition in mind, repurposing the story to "aid communication"—communication between the two women, and also communication between the play and the audience. I redirected attention on the ways in which both women had benefitted from imbalances in the relationship, and in the process I learned something about life and about myself. If the "scene" of a lifelong relationship is well-lit, assigning blame becomes a moot point. In the words of Emma Goldman, "Before we can forgive one another, we have to understand one another."

Jean's articulation of the higher purpose of lighting illuminated my own craft for me, and *Lighting Martha* became a play that was not about settling scores, but about compassion. It became a play affirming our capacity to heal in our relationships, even after the death of a partner.

Returning to this script, I could see so clearly that I did not have the maturity in my early fifties to take on the subject of dying. Over the last fifteen years, most of my mentors and many of my colleagues have died. I have attended services and written many memorials. My own mortality is no longer an abstraction, but a distinct, ever-present possibility. I have begun the process of putting my house in order, and part of that has included coming to terms with whom and what I have loved, and how I have expressed that love. The primary commitment has always been to the work—to the plays. In *Lighting Martha*, I plead my own case before some imaginary bar, that this love of, and total commitment to the art is also worthy and deserving, a counterweight against manifest deficiencies in relationship histories. In calling for compassion for my characters, I have become a beneficiary myself.

Female Nude Seated

Researching the life of Irish, lesbian painter Mainie Jellett, I became intrigued by the fact that she and her partner Evie Hone had both studied under Walter Sickert in 1917 at the Westminster School of Art. In two of her books, lesbian crime writer Patricia Cornwell makes a compelling case that Sickert was actually Jack the Ripper. Whether or not this is true, much of Sickert's art is focused on harsh and faceless depictions of naked, prostituted women in juxtaposition with fully clothed, potentially menacing johns. He titled a painting of his own living space "Jack the Ripper's Bedroom."

What is the impact on women, and especially on women who love women, of these profoundly misogynist mentors? I learned my craft in a male-dominated theatre department, studying a canon of work that was written entirely by male playwrights, and nearly always directed by males. The struggle for my identity in this environment was fierce, and in the end, I went "off the grid" to work with nothing but women in severely marginalized and stigmatized, women-only theatre companies for three decades. I wrote with a voice I had never heard on any stage. What was my experience? I quote Elizabeth Blackwell, the first woman to receive a medical degree in the US. "It is not easy to be a pioneer, but oh, it is fascinating! I would not trade one moment, even the worst moment, for all the riches in the world."

Mainie Jellett has been credited with revolutionizing art in Ireland. Ten years before Cubist Abstract works were shown in England, she was displaying them in Ireland. She and Evie left their art school in London to study with abstract painters in Paris. Returning home to Dublin, the two women became leading spiritual and cultural voices of the Irish Free State.

I was curious to explore potential connections between their studying with Sickert and their subsequent repudiation of representational art in favor of abstraction. I was also fascinated by what it may have been like to come of age in London in 1917. It would have been the third year of "The Great War," when the reports of horrendous carnage were beginning to undermine patriotic rhetoric about the glories of empire. By 1917, the boys who so proudly paraded off to war were filtering back to the streets of London with bandaged heads, crippled limbs, and tortured minds. Londoners who, in 1916, had gathered in the streets at the novelty of air raid sirens, curious to see what it was all about, were now huddling in terror in tube stations under the city.

The Russian Revolution, in part a reaction to the European war, had begun, and the Easter Rising of 1916 had birthed a militant movement for Irish independence. By 1917, the party of the Irish people, Sinn Féin, had committed itself to the establishment of an Irish Republic. Although the Suffragettes had officially suspended their activism for the sake of solidarity in the war effort, the national recruitment of women to fill jobs traditionally held by men had rapidly and radically transformed popular ideas about gender and gender roles, advancing the cause of women's liberation.

How would these social upheavals affect a young, middle-class Irish woman raised with traditional Protestant and Unionist values? Jellett's revolutionary art found its abstract roots in medieval art, and especially in Catholic motifs. Her partner Evie would convert to Catholicism and become one of the foremost stained-glass designers of the century. Not only did these women bring Modernism to Ireland, but together they restored the roots of a Celtic spiritual tradition to Irish art.

In my play, I also wanted to explore what it meant for a girl child to survive polio in turn-of-the century Ireland. Evie Hone, whose mother died in giving birth to her, was stricken at the age of eleven. In 1905, it was the accepted practice to take children with polio from their homes and to warehouse them in hospital wards, often for years. Only the parents—no siblings—were allowed to visit, and the visits were limited to communications between thick plate glass. Treatment consisted of full-torso plaster casts intended to keep the spine straight, splints for the limbs, and multiple, excruciating, and disfiguring surgeries for reattaching ligaments and tendons, and fusing and straightening bones. Although a member of the landed gentry, Evie's privilege would not have spared her from the ravages of the disease or the trauma of quarantine and multiple, largely ineffectual surgeries.

Female Nude Seated is a story of two young women at personal crossroads in their lives, at an extraordinary time of social change. I envisioned an evening that would mark the turning point for both women—artistically, sexually, and politically. Both women are in freefall. Planning individual escapes, they can no longer accommodate a world that has already become obsolete. At the same time, neither is prepared to forge a place for herself in the new world that is being birthed.

52 Pickup

I was reading a call for submissions for an anthology of short plays on the subject of suicide. The plays would also be performed in conjunction with National Suicide Prevention Week.

Suicide has touched my life in recent years with the death of two friends of mine. One of them was an especially close friend, and she attempted more than half a dozen times before completing. It was a painful journey for those of us who loved her.

I also made an attempt when I was a very young woman, more than forty-five years ago. I am still friends with the woman who was my primary support person at that time. I remember very little about that episode, but when we were discussing this play, she reminded me that she came to see me when I got home from the hospital and that we sat on the bed and played cards.

I believe in writing this play, I was wanting to reach back and take some responsibility for the people I hurt with my attempt… and I also wanted to vent some of the powerful and complicated emotions I still hold over the death of my friend.

The play did what I always hope a play will do: It took on a life of its own during the writing. As the characters of Janiya and Cil began to emerge, they elbowed me, as the writer, to the side. It became my job to get out of their way, to listen, and to record.

I began to realize that this play was never going to make it into that anthology… that it might never even make it to the stage. But it was telling a truth that was important to me, as a woman who has been on both sides of the act.

Lesbian poet Adrienne Rich wrote, "When a woman tells the truth, she is creating the possibility for more truth around her." When attempting suicide has become an obsession and a compulsive, repeated behavior, overt expressions of grief and rage can become repressed, and, in my experience, this repression results in cycles of reciprocal, escalating resentment—a resentment that fuels the ideation and behavior.

In this play, the use of the card game as a metaphor frees Cil to express the anger she has been repressing in the name of compassion. This anger breaks through Janiya's numbing alienation, powerfully reasserting connection to community. Unable to hide from it anymore, Janiya accesses the grief that underlies her own anger.

With both characters overwhelmed and emotionally spent, the play ends in the creation of healing space for humility and humanity.

Miss Le Gallienne Announces the New Season

I was invited to contribute to a collection of brief monologues about famous historical women from the world of theatre. Having already written a one-act about Eva Le Gallienne's backstage rape during a Broadway run and her subsequent founding of the Civic Repertory Theatre (*Entr'acte, or The Night Eva Le Gallienne Was Raped*), I initially struggled with the idea of a brief monologue. What could I say about this complicated, multi-talented, visionary artist in the space of three or four pages?

And then I remembered her gruesome, near-death experience from a propane explosion in her Connecticut home in 1931. I remembered how she left for Europe just a few months after it, and how she reopened the Civic Rep just a year later, with an ambitious season of producing, directing, and performing. Her badly burned hands were still healing, and so was she.

One of her biographers recounted an incident where Eva was re-traumatized by a photographer's setting off of a flashbulb, and how she lashed out in anger, throwing up her hands: *"Young man, you don't know what that means to me. I nearly lost my hands in an explosion. I'm really quite sick."*

Reading that quotation, I realized I had found a subject that was limited in scope (the fire, her hands, the press conference), but one that held fascination for me. Eva, by her own account still "quite sick," was nonetheless determined not to allow the accident to derail the freight-train momentum of her success with the Civic Rep. Later in life, Eva would describe this fire as the event that divided her life into two distinct parts: before the fire and after the fire, but in 1932 she was still treating it as "merely a flesh wound." It barely warranted a mention in the autobiography she was writing the year of her recovery, *At 33*.

Eva was known for her ability to "fascinate and beguile" reporters. I was interested in exploring a post-fire Eva attempting to reprise this pre-fire persona for a group of aggressively prying reporters. Trauma has a way of hijacking the narrative of victims who attempt to minimize or deny our experience of the event. I wanted to put this struggle on the stage. It is one that I have lived through more than two decades of touring.

I also wanted to explore the love-hate relationship between a celebrity and her public. The same members of the press who can bestow and perpetuate fame are also incentivized to uncover any scars and scandals attached to their subjects. Eva, with her scarred hands and traumatized psyche, enters the theatre like a lion-tamer entering the cage. Obviously outnumbered, her safety lies in avoiding any display of vulnerability, something a polished performer can certainly pull off—except for the wildcard of PTSD, Post-Traumatic Stress Disorder.

I struggled for an empowering ending, feeling that Eva would need to pull herself together for a satisfying finish. In fact, what I want to say is that it is a great watershed in recovery, when we survivors finally give up the fight for the life we were living before and surrender to the journey of healing. It is empowering when we give up managing the impressions of others to grieve our losses and to stand in alliance with, instead of in defiance of, our disabilities and our disfigurements. And if my audiences reject this ending, perhaps, when the day comes—as it will, in all likelihood—when they find themselves permanently altered by catastrophe, they may remember this play and its ending in a different light.

Black Star

A Play About Henrietta Vinton Davis

Cast of Characters

HENRIETTA VINTON DAVIS: African American woman, 64.

ROBERT LINCOLN POSTON: African American man, mid-30's, extremely well-dressed.

YOUNG HENRIETTA: A younger version of HENRIETTA, 30's.

*JAMES: Young male, stage manager. 20's.

*POWHATAN BEATY: African American man, 40's.

*THOMAS SYMMONS: African American male, late 30's. Cheap, natty dresser.

*FREDERICK DOUGLASS: African American male, 75.

MISS TAYLOR: Bi-racial, former chorus girl, 16.

*WILL MARION COOK: African American male, 24, expensively dressed.

*BENNY DANCY: Older African American male, wears a worn, but immaculate suit.

*The roles of Powhatan Beaty, Frederick Douglass, and Benny Dancy may be performed by one actor. The roles of James, Will Marion Cook, and Thomas Symmons may be played by one actor.

Scene Synopsis

Act I

Scene 1: A backstage dressing room in Liberty Hall, Harlem, August 24, 1924.

Scene 2: A backstage dressing room at the Ford Theatre, Washington, DC, April 1884.

Scene 3: Same as Scene 1.

Scene 4: A backstage dressing room in a theatre in Cincinatti, Ohio, 1893.

Scene 5: Same as Scene 1.

Scene 6: A backstage dressing room in a theatre in Chicago, 1893.

Scene 7: Same as Scene 1.

Scene 8: An antechamber in the courthouse for the United States Court of Appeals for the Second Circuit, lower Manhattan, May 1923

Scene 9: Same as Scene 1.

Black Star

Scene 1

*Lights come up on a dressing room, backstage at
Liberty Hall in Harlem. The room has a makeup
mirror, a chair, a table, and a folding screen for
changing clothing. It is August 24, 1924, during the
third international convention of the United Negro
Improvement Association (UNIA). HENRIETTA
VINTON DAVIS is preparing to make an entrance.
HENRIETTA is an African American woman, 64,
dressed in a floor-length gown. She is looking over her
notes as she performs last-minute touch-ups with her
hair and gown.*

HENRIETTA: *(Practicing her speech to the mirror.)* "I
esteem it a very great honor to have the pleasure of
introducing to you the man of the hour…"*(She stops, checks
her watch, touches up her lipstick, and starts over, speaking
more rapidly.)* "I esteem it a very great honor to have the
pleasure of introducing to you the man of the hour… *(More
lipstick. She speaks rapidly, in a distracted and agitated
manner. This is a memorized speech.)* …the man who has
stood upon the Olympian heights, who has caught the vision
of the gods for his people, whose clarion voice has been
echoed from mountaintop to mountaintop until it has circled
the globe, calling his brothers to arms. That man is the
undaunted, the unconquerable, the incomparable *Marcus
Garvey…*" *(She pats her hair one more time, crosses to the
door and begins to open it. Suddenly the lights go out. When
they come back on, they are either dimmed or gelled, giving
off an eerie light. HENRIETTA tries the door. It's locked.
Rattling the door.)* What's going on…? Hello..? Someone
open the door… Open the door… please… It's locked… I
can't get out… *(She begins banging.)* Hello…? The dressing

4

room door is *locked*! *(Suddenly a figure steps out from behind the screen. This is the ghost of ROBERT LINCOLN POSTON, an African American man, 33. He is extremely well-dressed.)*

ROBERT: Hello, Henrietta.

HENRIETTA: *(Turning and freezing in shock.)* No! *(A pause. She shakes her head.)* Oh, no… Oh, no… I do *not* have time for this! I have a speech to give. *(She turns back to the door, banging on it with renewed vigor.)* Help! Somebody… Anybody! Open the door! Open this door! Help! Help…! *(More banging. Patiently, ROBERT waits. Finally, HENRIETTA turns back to him.)* I am *not* talking to you! *(ROBERT sits casually and crosses his legs. HENRIETTA goes back to banging on the door.)* Open this door! Open the door! *(Finally, she turns to ROBERT.)* Unlock this door.

ROBERT: What makes you think I locked it?

HENRIETTA: Robert Lincoln Poston, you let me go out there and introduce Mr. Garvey. There are six thousand people at this convention—six thousand members of the Universal Negro Improvement Association—and they are waiting for me to introduce their president and then to give my report…

ROBERT: *(Smiling.)* Ah, yes… *your* report.

HENRIETTA: You open this door right now, or else I'm going to—

ROBERT: What are you going to do, Henrietta… kill me? *(He pauses.)* You know I'm already dead… *(Pause.)* In fact, you were there when I died…

HENRIETTA: *(Frightened, she begins to look through her notes, attempting to ground.)* This isn't real. *(Pause.)* This is *not* real.

ROBERT: Well, now we're starting to get somewhere. *(She looks at him.)* The great Henrietta Vinton Davis admitting something is not real.

HENRIETTA: *(Shaking her head.)* Oh, no, Robert. Oh, no… I am *not* going there with you…

ROBERT: *(Shrugging.)* Well, apparently you are not going anywhere.

HENRIETTA: *(Looking around the room.)* We're not at Liberty Hall anymore, are we? *(Pause.)* This isn't even Harlem, is it? *(Pause. She checks her watch.)* And time has stopped… This must be a dream.

ROBERT: Or maybe *that*, out there, is the dream…? Marcus Garvey…? *(With sarcasm.)* The great "African Redemption?" The Universal Negro Improvement Association… ? Maybe *this* is the reality. Hmm? The place where people go when they can't tell the difference between truth and a lie anymore…?

HENRIETTA: *(Exasperated.)* Oh, my God, Robert! What the hell do you want?

ROBERT: *(Suddenly serious and angry.)* I want you to tell the truth.

HENRIETTA: And what truth is that? The one that killed you? Dead at thirty-three, Robert. Look, I'm sixty-four and *I'm* still here.

ROBERT: *(Very angry.)* No, Henrietta, it was *his* lies— Marcus Garvey's lies—*your* lies that killed me! And I'm not going to let you walk out there and keep telling those same lies to my brothers and sisters. Lies! Lies to make them open their wallets and their purses and drop their hard-earned wages into the plate for some half-assed, bullshit pipedream about a fleet of ocean liners owned by Blacks, navigated by Blacks, stem-to-stern booked with Black passengers… a fleet of second-hand, leaky, rust-bucket freighters that is supposed to carry half the country back to "the Motherland"—to some mythical Dahomey—to some Africa dreamed up in the mind of a Jamaican snake oil salesman—an Africa that you know as well as I do does not exist, because *we were just there. (She turns away.)* We were *there*, Henrietta, six months ago… Dammit, look at me!

HENRIETTA: *(Uncomfortable.) Yes*, we were there… so…? *(Rallying.)* And you got sick on the way home, and you died on that ship… You're *dead*, Robert Poston! I don't know why you are here!

ROBERT: You know exactly why I'm here, because we were in that damned Liberian delegation together. And it was all a lie! That whole delegation… It was just a lie … an excuse to raise more money. Garvey telling the world how he was sending delegates—you and me!—over to Africa to finalize the arrangements for a mass emigration to Liberia! "Finalize the arrangements!" What arrangements? The ones he made up in his head? The President of Liberia must have thought we were crazy… knocking on his door to see if he would mind if we moved into his house… us and a hundred thousand of our friends. *(In a fury.)* He's not even going to let Garvey's ships dock in his port… assuming they could actually make the crossing!

HENRIETTA: *(Quietly.)* The President of Liberia went back on his word. You know that was because DuBois—

ROBERT: No, Henrietta! No! Not everything is a damn conspiracy!

HENRIETTA: Well, *that* was, and you know it! Mr. Garvey had already raised two million dollars—

ROBERT: Really? Two million? Did you ever see that money? Did anyone *ever* see any of the money that made it into the donation buckets?

HENRIETTA: I *hope*—I sincerely *hope*—that you are not suggesting that Mr. Garvey is a thief. Careless as he may be with his bookkeeping, he is not a thief! Every penny goes into the United Negro Improvement Association, and anyone who knows Mr. Garvey understands that.

ROBERT: Careless, because he doesn't care. It's all for show!

HENRIETTA: I don't understand where this is coming from. You were in the UNIA administration... While you were alive, I never heard you talk like this—

ROBERT: Well, sometimes it takes dying to see the light.

HENRIETTA: What light? India is fighting for their national freedom. Ireland is fighting for their national freedom. Why not Africa for Africans? Why not? And why is it such a fantasy for us to go back? Listen, Robert, the year I was born, right in my home state Maryland, they passed a bill to send us all back to Africa. Every single adult Black—free *and* slave— in Maryland... just put us all on a ship back to Africa! Oh, but not our childen... they would be left behind as slaves. They *passed* that bill—in *my* lifetime, Robert! They *passed* that damn bill, and if it hadn't been for my stepfather giving speeches and circulating petitions and raising hell for a general election, they would have enforced it. If it's something white people want, it's a law, but if it's something *we* want... then it's fantasy... snake oil! And why can't we own a steamship line? Sixty years ago in Baltimore there was an all-Black shipbuilding company. If we can build them, why can't we own them?

ROBERT: Henrietta, wake up! Marcus Garvey doesn't know the first thing about politics or boats! He doesn't know anything and he doesn't care! He gives speeches! That's what he does. Marcus Garvey gives speeches and people believe him, because he tells them something they want to hear. He's a hustler! Who is the man? He came up here from Jamaica, out of nowhere… up to Harlem and he sees fruit ripe for the picking! And now he's got people they trust… like you… famous Shakespearean actress… and what are you doing? Selling fake stock certificates for the Black Star steamship line—

HENRIETTA: *(Quietly.)* They aren't fake and I *don't* sell them anymore. Mr. Garvey has dissolved the Black Star Line.

ROBERT: Only because he got busted!

HENRIETTA: He was set up! You know that! Mail fraud! That whole trial was a kangaroo court—

ROBERT: But you're *still* hawking those damn steamships! All Garvey did was change the name of the company and now, instead of selling stock, he's asking people straight up for *loans*… They don't even get the fake stock certificate! *Nothing* to show for the money. *Nothing*!

 HENRIETTA: Well, Robert, you used to believe—

ROBERT: Yes, I did, and I died for that belief, and this is my redemption, Henrietta. This is *my* "African Redemption"—not letting you go out there and tell any more lies! So, welcome to limbo, Henrietta. Might as well put your feet up, because you're going to be here a while.

HENRIETTA: *(Rallying.)* No, I'm not! Because I know what this is… I was not born yesterday! This is *harassment*. And you are a *heckler*. Unh-huh. That is what you are, and that is *all* you are! A heckler! Dead or not, you are nothing but a two-bit troublemaker from the peanut gallery—upstaging me with this locked-door stunt, because that is *all* you've got. Well, I did not spend four decades of my life performing on the stages of the greatest cities on this continent with the most legendary actors of our race to be upstaged by a *dead man*. And you are not the only one who can play with time and place! You are not the only conjurer in the house tonight! Conjuring is my stock-in-trade. *(She turns to front of the stage.)* We are going back forty years in time tonight. Forty years back, to the Ford Opera House in Washington, DC! It's 1884. *(She turns to ROBERT.)* I'm going to show you what I do to hecklers…

Blackout

End of Scene

Scene 2

The lights come up in a dressing room at the Ford Theatre in Washington, DC, 1884. A young woman dressed as Lady Macbeth storms into the room. This is YOUNG HENRIETTA, 24. She is followed closely by JAMES, a young and very distraught stage manager.

JAMES: But Miss Davis, what am I going to tell them?

YOUNG HENRIETTA: *(Enraged.)* When the intermission is over, you tell them that *Macbeth* has been cancelled, that they can get their hats and coats and go home.

JAMES: I can't do that!

YOUNG HENRIETTA: Then don't! Let them sit there until hell freezes over. I don't care!

JAMES: But, Miss Davis—

YOUNG HENRIETTA: *(Cutting him off.)* Excuse me. *(She pushes him out and closes the door.)*

JAMES: *(Offstage.)* Miss Davis… Miss Davis! *(YOUNG HENRIETTA throws off her queenly cape and turns to the mirror. Voices are heard offstage. Knocking.)*

YOUNG HENRIETTA: I said go away! I don't care!

POWHATAN BEATY: *(Offstage.)* Henrietta…

YOUNG HENRIETTA: Go away!

POWHATAN BEATY: *(Offstage.)* It's Powhatan Beaty…

YOUNG HENRIETTA: *(Jumping up and opening the door.)* I'm sorry, Mr. Beaty… I thought you were the stage manager. *(POWHATAN BEATY enters. He is an African American man in his late forties, nearly twice the age of YOUNG HENRIETTA. He wears the costume of Macbeth and speaks with a trained, stentorian voice.)*

POWHATAN BEATY: What's this about cancelling the show?

YOUNG HENRIETTA: I'm sorry, but I've made up my mind.

POWHATAN BEATY: Because…

YOUNG HENRIETTA: Because I am the producer and I can. *(He waits.)* Because I am not going to allow my actors to perform under these conditions. *(He waits. She explodes.)* You heard the audience out there! Hooting and whistling and making noises like chimpanzees…

POWHATAN BEATY: Not all of them… Henrietta, there's eleven hundred people out there.

YOUNG HENRIETTA: *(Angry.)* If I wanted to make a fool of myself on the stage, I would have joined a minstrel show or I'd be touring in *Uncle Tom's Cabin*! I wouldn't have hired Powhatan Beaty to play *Macbeth* and I wouldn't have leased Ford's Theatre! *(Turning to him.)* This is the theatre where Lincoln was shot!

POWHATAN BEATY: *(Smiling.)* Yes, and imagine how *he* felt about that…

YOUNG HENRIETTA: You know who is out there? Frederick Douglass! Frederick Douglass… I used to work for him at the copyright office. He was the one who told me to go and live my dream of being a performer. He was the one who pushed me… On my first night, he invited his friends and he got up on the stage and introduced me… I can't let him see me humiliated like this.

POWHATAN BEATY: Do you think you're the first Black actor who ever got harassed?

YOUNG HENRIETTA: I don't care! Maybe I'm the first who won't put up with it. *(POWHATAN shakes his head. This infuriates her.) I* wasn't born in slavery!

POWHATAN BEATY: *(Turning to face her.)* I see… *(There is a long and awkward silence.)*

YOUNG HENRIETTA: *(Embarrassed.)* I just mean that—

POWHATAN BEATY: *(Speaking slowly, with deliberation.)* Oh, I understand what you mean, and I think, Miss Davis, you had better go back to your copyright office. *(He turns to leave.)*

YOUNG HENRIETTA: Mr. Beaty—

POWHATAN BEATY: *(Turning back.)* You know something, Henrietta… If you *had* been born in slavery, you would "screw your courage to the sticking place" right now, instead of quitting. *(A pause.)* You know what that means, don't you? *(Silence.)* You don't? *(He shakes his head in disbelief.)* People pay you their good money to hear you speak those lines as Lady Macbeth, and you don't even know what they mean… mmm. *(Shaking his head, he turns to exit.)*

YOUNG HENRIETTA: Mr. Beaty, wait… Please. I'm sorry… I'm sorry. *(A long pause.)* Tell me… about the "sticking place."

POWHATAN BEATY: *(He considers before he turns to answer her.)* The sticking place is part of a crossbow. You *do* know what a crossbow is? *(Ashamed, she nods.)* Well, the sticking place holds the peg that holds the bowstring. You pull that string as far back as you possibly can… *(Miming the action.)*… and then you screw the peg down to the sticking place. So, you see, now you're all loaded up and ready to go. All you have to do is aim and release. Because it's pretty hard to aim at the same time you're holding all that tension in your arm. *(She looks at him.)*

Well, that's what Lady Macbeth is saying… That if she and her husband just pull up and screw their courage to the sticking place, they can't fail. You see, the crossbow really switched up the odds in a battle. Before the crossbow, it took a lot of skill, a lot of muscle to be any good with a bow and arrow. But then the crossbow came along, and pretty much anybody could be dangerous… even you, Henrietta Davis. *(He has her attention now.)*

What we do in these dressing rooms, is we stretch our memories back just like we are pulling on a crossbow string. *(Crossing away from her.)* I come into a dressing room, like this one tonight, and I take a deep breath… *(He illustrates.)* …and then I start pulling that memory string back… back past the latest indignity… past the last train station I had to sleep in because there were no hotels for coloreds, past the last pocketful of hard-boiled eggs I had to eat for dinner, because there were no restaurants that would seat me, past that last time I took my life in my hands, just to use a bathroom, because there wasn't a second one specially marked for me.

And then I start pulling back even farther. I stretch that memory back to the war, back to the Battle of Chaffin's Farm, when our standard-bearer got shot, and I ran six hundred yards through enemy fire to retrieve our flag—six hundred yards, Henrietta, six hundred yards where every breath was my last... just to snag that raggedy piece of cloth so covered in mud nobody would even recognize it. Because it stood for something. And this is when I really start pulling. I haul my memory back over those two decades of living hell, when a white man owned me, and owned my family... and all the way back to when my grandparents were taken in Africa and forced onto a ship. And— do you know what a windlass its? *(She shakes her head.)* It's a kind of crank with pulleys that people use when they need to move something that's just too heavy for them to bear. People use a windlass on the crossbow to get that string further back than a single human arm can pull it. So, now I get that windlass of *ancestral* memory cranking... and now I am pulling all the way back to the kingdoms of Dahomey and Aruba, back to that time when we were kings and queens... emperors... *(Picking up her discarded robe.) ...and* empresses... *(He drapes the robe over YOUNG HENRIETTA and turns her gently toward the mirror.)* Rulers on our own continent, on a Black continent... back to when we had our own empires... back to the Mali Empire, the Ashanti Empire... back to Nubia, Axum, Carthage, Ghana, Mali, Songhay... back—way back—before the Greeks and before the Romans... back to the Great Pyramids of Giza, the Temple of Karnak, ... And *then,* and *only* then, I screw that memory down to the sticking place.

So, now, Henrietta... *(She turns back to him, away from the mirror. As he speaks she crosses down behind him, with a new sense of dignity and purpose, his pupil. She follows him as he crosses to the front of the stage.) Now*, now that I've got my memory stretched taut and screwed down... *now*, I can walk out on that stage free and easy. Now, I can take my time to aim my arrow, because I'm not working against myself anymore. I don't have to bother about their taunts or their catcalls, because all I have to do is pull that little pin out of the "sticking place..." I just release that, and my words fly out with the force of two hundred *thousand* years of history, one hundred *million* African voices... across four *thousand* miles of Middle Passage… and six hundred yards of Mr. Chaffin's farm. *(A long silence. Suddenly, there is a knock on the door.)*

JAMES: *(Offstage.)* Miss Davis… *(POWHATAN turns and looks at her. YOUNG HENRIETTA crosses to the door and opens it. JAMES enters.)* The intermission is almost over—

YOUNG HENRIETTA: Well, then call "places" for the second act.

JAMES: But…

YOUNG HENRIETTA: Places!

JAMES: *(Confused, turns to POWHATAN.)* But, she said—

POWHATAN BEATY: Places!

JAMES: *(He turns back to YOUNG HENRIETTA. Finally, he throws up his arms and exits.)* Places!

POWHATAN BEATY: *(Offering his arm.)* Lady Macbeth…?

YOUNG HENRIETTA: *(Taking it.)* Milord. *(They exit.)*

Blackout

End of Scene

Scene 3

Lights come up on the dressing room at Liberty Hall, the same as in Scene 1. HENRIETTA and ROBERT stare at each other for a moment.

ROBERT: *(He begins to clap very slowly. She stares at him until he stops.)* Very dramatic… Not too sure about the point—

HENRIETTA: The *point* is I know how to deal with hecklers. I learned from the best. *(She tries the door again. Still locked.)*

ROBERT: *(Nodding.)* I see… And are *all* your memories theatre?

HENRIETTA: What do you mean?

ROBERT: Oh, like that… Heroic, swashbuckling, grandiloquent, good-triumphing-over-evil… you know… Garvey-ite bullshit?

HENRIETTA: *(Turning slowly.)* Now, see, *this* is heckling.

ROBERT: Oh, and is that what you call reality when it intrudes on your fantasies?

HENRIETTA: I appreciate Mr. Garvey in ways that you cannot, because I also am a performer.

ROBERT: So you admit it's all theatre?

HENRIETTA: Of course. What did you think it was? *(Pause. She looks at ROBERT.)* Now *you* disappoint *me*, Robert. All those pageants and parades through Harlem… the Universal African Legion honor guard, and the Black Cross nurses, and the African Motor Corps, and the choirs, and the marching

17

bands… and all that regalia… my god!—the ceremonial swords, and the sashes, and the epaulets, and the bandoliers… oh, and the hat… the hat with the cockade and the plumes— like he was Napoleon! Tell me you didn't think that hat was a costume! *(ROBERT tries to break in, but she cuts him off.)* And the *titles*! "Provincial President of Africa." He named himself president of a whole continent. *President.* The man never even set foot there. And he knighted me … Do you remember that? "Lady Commander of the Sublime Order of the Nile." How the hell did you *not* know it was theatre…?

ROBERT: And you *still* believe him?

HENRIETTA: No, Robert. I believe *in* him. Which is a different thing. I have spent my career attempting to create a world on the stage, and, if I was good… I mean, if I was *really* good, I might be able to bring my audiences into my reality for an hour or two—for the duration of the play. But what Mr. Garvey is doing is creating a world without a stage—*without* a stage!… right up here in Harlem… and he is bringing the Blacks of the world, of the *whole* world—*millions*—into that world and he is schooling us, *rehearsing* us on how to live there.

ROBERT: *(Angry.)* He's lying to you and to all his followers, and you are lying to yourselves!

HENRIETTA: *(Ignoring ROBERT's outburst.)* Here's the thing about theatre… It looks real. It feels real. It has a taste… a taste of freedom, of dignity… a taste of grandeur. And so when that curtain comes down and the "real world," as you call it, comes to take us back… well, see, we're not so docile now. We've had that taste and it makes us want to fight. I have *been* Lady Macbeth. I have *been* Cleopatra, Empress of Africa. Yes, only for an hour or two and, yes, on a stage. But it changed me. And all of those uniforms and all those pageants—

ROBERT: *(Cutting her off.)* Oh, save it! Save the speeches for your audience. Oh, wait… that's right… You don't have one! You're trapped in your dressing room… with a ghost!

HENRIETTA: Shut up, Robert! You're dead, and, see, that's the thing about being dead… You lose your turn! *(Shrugging, ROBERT takes out a deck of cards and begins to deal out a solitaire game. HENRIETTA tries the door again. Frustrated, she turns and watches him.)* All right. Let's look at this precious truth of yours. *(He looks up briefly.)*

ROBERT: Five-card? *(Surprised, she hesitates and then sits. ROBERT begins to deal the first round of five-card stud: one card down and one card up.)*

HENRIETTA: *(Sitting.)* If I'm remembering rightly, after Howard University, you went to Princeton.

ROBERT: That's right… Shall we make it interesting?

HENRIETTA: *(Removing her watch and placing between them.)* There's no time here, anyway. *(ROBERT takes off his wedding ring.)* Your wedding ring…?

ROBERT: *(With bitter irony.)* Death us did part.

HENRIETTA: So, at Princeton you pitched a fit and got yourself thrown out.

ROBERT: *(Dealing the second round: one card face up.)* They let us take the courses, but they wouldn't give us our degrees. *(He takes off one cufflink.)* Cufflink.

HENRIETTA: I'll see you an earring. *(She puts in an earring.)* And so after Princeton, you went and enlisted—

ROBERT: *(Dealing the third round: one card face up.)* Made sergeant in three days... *(He removes his second cufflink.)* Cufflink.

HENRIETTA: *(Removing an earring.)* Earring. But they kicked you out of there, too.

ROBERT: *Discharged* me. *(He deals the final round: one card face down.)* I sued the army over their treatment of Black soldiers.

HENRIETTA: *(Studying her cards.)* Well, that's the last of my jewelry... What do you say, we play for some real stakes now...? *(She opens her purse.)*

ROBERT: No money... as useless as time.

HENRIETTA: *(Taking out a piece of folded paper.)* Better than money.

ROBERT: What is it?

HENRIETTA: You'll have to win first.

ROBERT: *(Taking out his wallet.)* Here. *(He removes a small photograph.)* Augusta... my wife... Not even married a year... *(He places the photo in the middle and begins to look at his cards. HENRIETTA stops him, putting her hand over his.)*

HENRIETTA: So, after the army, you went home and started a newspaper, but you quit that, too...

ROBERT: *(Watching her eyes. HENRIETTA keeps her hand on his.)* I published an editorial about the local Fourth of July parade... about how the Black veterans had to march in back.

HENRIETTA: So. Princeton, the Army, and…

ROBERT: *(Smiling.) The Hopkinsville Contender.*

HENRIETTA: You quit all of them.

ROBERT: Was forced to.

HENRIETTA: But you didn't see any of that coming…? *(A long pause. A showdown.)* Well, I'm puzzled by that, Robert. Because if you didn't see it coming, you must have been very stupid… but I know that you're not. But if you *did* see it coming, then it all seems very self-destructive.

ROBERT: Nothing changes if nothing changes.

HENRIETTA: So you thought you were going to change white people?

ROBERT: Maybe. *(HENRIETTA removes her hand.)*

HENRIETTA: But Garvey's the fantasist…?

ROBERT: *(Turning over his cards.)* One pair.

HENRIETTA: *(Turning over hers.)* Flush.

ROBERT: All yours…

HENRIETTA: Only one thing in the pile that's any use to me… *(She retrieves the folded paper and places it back in her purse.)*

ROBERT: *(Taking back the ring and photo.)* I don't get to know what it is?

HENRIETTA: You lost. And you're dead. And that's because you were in a hurry. You just couldn't stand to see your potential wasted. And when you couldn't get white people to change fast enough for you, you signed on with Mr. Garvey, because he wasn't talking about changing them. He was talking about sailing off to a new world. And you just couldn't wait for that world... one without white people, one where everything would be just the way you always imagined it... And when *that* didn't happen quite as fast as you needed it to, it broke your spirit. Just snapped it in two. I was there. I saw it...Just snapped you right in two. It wasn't pneumonia that killed you, Robert Poston. It was your own busted dreams. You just couldn't wait.

ROBERT: So why don't you go out there and give those six thousand people a lecture on patience... Go out there and tell them that the world they are so desperate to find is going to take time. Time they won't live to see. But you can't do that, can you? Because that's not what they came to hear. They're all in a hurry, too... just like I was. Otherwise, they would be down in Tuskegee learning the fine art of brickmaking or up in Manhattan with Mr. DuBois and his precious "talented tenth." Maybe *you* understand that it's all theatre... but do they? *(Seeing where this is going, HENRIETTA grabs her purse and tries to leave again. The door is still locked.)*

HENRIETTA: This is heckling.

ROBERT: No, Henrietta, it's not. I'm not here to bother the actor. I'm here to shut down the whole show. *(HENRIETTA tries the door again. It is still locked. ROBERT crosses behind her.)* You are choosing, eyes wide open, to give your time and your money to Mr. Garvey, but they are not. You're going to break their purses and then their hearts, Henrietta. Every single one of them! You're going to murder them all!

HENRIETTA: *(Reaching into her purse, she pulls out a small pocket pistol, whirls around, and aims it at ROBERT.)* You're not the first man who ever tried to break me. Cincinnati! 1893!

Blackout

End of Scene

Scene 4

Lights come up on a dressing room in a Cincinnati theatre, 1893. YOUNG HENRIETTA, 33, is sitting at a dressing table in a robe, putting up her hair. A fancy gown is draped over the back of a chair. Next to this chair is her purse. Suddenly THOMAS SYMMONS stumbles in drunk. He is in his 40's, a flashy dresser. He has been her manager/husband for ten years.

YOUNG HENRIETTA: *(Startled.)* Oh, my god! Tommy, you scared me to death… *(Realizing his condition.)* What do you want?

THOMAS: Can't a man visit his own wife?

YOUNG HENRIETTA: *(Exasperated.)* I have a show in fifteen minutes—

THOMAS: *(Cutting her off, with an edge.)* I know that! I *got* you this booking, didn't I? I'm your *manager*, or did you forget…?

YOUNG HENRIETTA: I need to get dressed now. *(Crossing to the dress on the chair. Turning pointedly to him.)* I'll see you after the show.

THOMAS: *(Pointing to the dress.)* Go ahead, darlin'. I don't mind. Ain't nothin' I haven't seen—

YOUNG HENRIETTA: *(Cutting him off.)* Is it money? Is that what you want? *(She takes out her purse.)*

THOMAS: Just hand me over the whole thing.

YOUNG HENRIETTA: I can't do that.

THOMAS: Yes, you can.

YOUNG HENRIETTA: No, I can't.

THOMAS: Why not?

YOUNG HENRIETTA: Look, here's five dollars. *(Offering it to him.)*

THOMAS: *(Not taking it.)* Why *not*? I'm your *manager*. I should *manage* the money. I used to do that.

YOUNG HENRIETTA: *(A wry smile.)* You used to do a lot of things.

THOMAS: *(Suddenly angry, he shoves her.)* Yeah, and you used to do a lot of things, too. Remember that!

YOUNG HENRIETTA: *(Quietly.)* I do remember.

THOMAS: *(Belligerently.)* *What*? What do you remember?

YOUNG HENRIETTA: *(Appeasing.)* Well… I remember that you used to sing. You were a singer—

THOMAS: And I gave it up for you! I gave up everything for you. *(He reaches for the purse. She moves it away. He escalates.)* *Everything*! So I could build you into a star. I made you, woman! I made you! Do you remember that? How I had to call in all my favors for you… They would shake their heads and say, "*Shakespeare*, Tommy…? I dunno… I dunno. Does she sing?" And I would say, "Man, she's does better than sing. She makes *you* sing… and not just with your mouth. She's gonna make you sing with every bone in your body… sing with pride and hope and glory." And they would shake their heads, "I dunno, Tommy." But I made 'em. Didn't I make 'em? Didn't I make 'em bring you in?

YOUNG HENRIETTA: Yes, that you did.

THOMAS: Don't you forget it.

YOUNG HENRIETTA: I don't.

THOMAS: And didn't I get you this booking in Cincinnati? And the one in Chicago before that… and Buffalo?

YOUNG HENRIETTA: *(Rising and leading him gently toward the door.)* Go on.

THOMAS: *(Shoving her.)* No!

YOUNG HENRIETTA: Tommy, I have to get dressed. *(He grabs the gown out of her hand and rips it. She responds with weariness.)* Well, that was not smart. I'm going to have to pay for that now, and I'm going to take it out of your liquor money.

THOMAS: It's *all* my money! I'm your manager.

YOUNG HENRIETTA: *(Really angry.)* No, it's not! And *you're* not. And you haven't been for years.

THOMAS: Years? *(Ticking them off on his fingers.)* Chicago, Detroit, Buffalo—

YOUNG HENRIETTA: Thomas, listen to me! *I* have been getting those bookings. *(He looks confused.)* Yes… *(Ticking them off on her fingers)* "Chicago, Detroit, Buffalo"… and before that *(More finger-ticking.)* Washington, and Philadelphia—

THOMAS: Liar! They come to me!

YOUNG HENRIETTA: They come to you, because I *send* them to you. *(He is stunned.)* I send them to you so you can pretend to be a manager. So you can pretend to be a man! *(He punches her, grabs her purse, and starts to exit.)*

THOMAS: *(Turning back.)* You see how far you get... a Black woman out on the road all by herself! *(He laughs.)* You just see how far you get without me... You see what kind of reputation you're going to have! Bitch! *(He exits. Wearily, she turns to the mirror to repair the damage.)*

Blackout

End of Scene

<h1 style="text-align:center">Scene 5</h1>

Lights come up on the dressing room at Liberty Hall, the same as in Scene 4. HENRIETTA is still holding a gun on ROBERT.

ROBERT: So… did you shoot your husband?

HENRIETTA: I didn't have to. *(Pointedly.)* He left.

ROBERT: Well, I'm not leaving.

HENRIETTA: Oh, yes, you are… go on. *(She crosses behind him and pushes the pistol into his back. ROBERT doesn't move.)* I said "go!" *(Pause.)* Then I guess I will have to kill you. *(She raises the gun to the back of his head.)*

ROBERT: I wouldn't do that, if I were you…

HENRIETTA: They can't hang me for shooting a man if he's already dead.

ROBERT: Listen to yourself, Henrietta! If I'm already dead, how can I still be standing here and talking to you? If I'm dead, whose spirit do you think is animating me?

HENRIETTA: *(After a long pause.)* Mine…? *(Slowly, she lowers the gun.)*

ROBERT: Dangerous thing, murdering a ghost… What are you going to exorcise… your memory…? your conscience…? I'd be very careful if I were you… *(HENRIETTA sits slowly at the makeup table and looks into the mirror. She keeps the gun with her. ROBERT takes the chair next to her, speaking gently.)* It's over. The show is over. And you gave a great performance. You really did. You sold a lot of people on a really beautiful dream. It *was* beautiful. Our own land, our own government... and those ships... those beautiful, gleaming ships, carrying all those families... I see them on the decks, leaning over the railings—the men in their suits and the women with their Sunday hats, holding onto the children who are laughing and throwing confetti, and everyone is waving good-bye... good-bye... But it's over, Henrietta... It's over. You have to go out there and tell them now. *(Pause.)* You go out and you take your bow and you send them home— to Harlem, not Africa. It was a good run—a great run. It was. You gave them a hell of a show, and they love you for it. But it's over, and it's time to stop now. *(He unfolds a piece of paper and puts it in front of her.)*

HENRIETTA: *(Alarmed.)* What's this?

ROBERT: You know what it is. You know *exactly* what it is...

HENRIETTA: *(Frightened, she jumps up.)* No! Chicago! Chicago 1893!

Blackout

End of Scene

Scene 6

Lights come up on a dressing room in a Chicago theatre, January 1893. YOUNG HENRIETTA sits in the dressing room that is doubling as an office, reading through a pile of manuscripts. The room is poorly heated, and she wears a scarf and keeps stopping to warm her fingers. There is a soft knock on the door.

YOUNG HENRIETTA: *(Not looking up.)* Come in… *(FREDERICK DOUGLASS, 75, enters. He is very well-dressed and carries a satchel.)*

FREDERICK: Henrietta! *(She turns around and stares.)* Henrietta Vinton Davis!

YOUNG HENRIETTA: Oh, my lord…

FREDERICK: You look like you're back at the copyright office.

YOUNG HENRIETTA: *(Rising.)* Mr. Douglass…! What are you doing in Chicago?

FREDERICK: I might ask you the same… *(He begins to take off his coat.)*

YOUNG HENRIETTA: Oh, don't take your coat off! I can't afford to heat the dressing rooms.

FREDERICK: *(Ignoring her, he removes his coat, sits and takes her hands.)* Now, what's this I hear… you and Thomas…?

YOUNG HENRIETTA: He's gone… He's gone, and it's good… No, really, it's good….I should have run that polecat off ten years ago!

FREDERICK: *(Indicating the space.)* But now you have your own theatre… Congratulations!

YOUNG HENRIETTA: I wish it *was* mine. I'm just renting, and that won't be for long if I don't come up with a show that can compete with the great Chicago world's fair.

FREDERICK: Well, I don't think that you need to worry about the Columbian Exposition. You know there's a boycott.

YOUNG HENRIETTA: I *do* know. I've got copies of your pamphlet right here. We've been handing them out in the theatre. *(She hands him one.)*

FREDERICK: *(Reading slowly.)* *"The Reason Why the Colored American Is Not in The World's Columbian Exposition."*

YOUNG HENRIETTA: I just don't know how effective it's going to be.

FREDICK: Title too long?

YOUNG HENRIETTA: *(Laughing.)* No. I think that you're asking a lot from people…

FREDERICK: Is it asking too much to boycott an event that completely excludes us… pretends we don't' even exist? They are calling it "A Century of Progress?" but they don't want to say who has made the most progress in this country in the last hundred years—hell, in the last thirty! Up from slavery! Hell, we *built* this country!

YOUNG HENRIETTA: *(A long pause.)* You *do* know they have a Ferris wheel, a moveable sidewalk, a cemetery of real mummies, the Liberty Bell, an Eskimo village, a live volcano, some… some… hoochie coochie dancer—

FREDERICK: "Little Egypt…?"

YOUNG HENRIETTA: *(Nodding.)* "Little Egypt." *(She stops abruptly and sighs.)* And if that isn't enough to sink my theatre, there's a new impresario in town—Sam T. Jack—and he's brought in his burlesque from New York—*The Creole Show*. Packing the house six nights a week—Black *and* white! Look! He's got his handbills all over Chicago. *(She hands him a handbill.)* Mr. Jack has just bought his own theatre, and I can't even make rent!

FREDERICK: *(Reading.)* "Fifty bewilderingly beautiful, divinely dashing, charming Creole ladies… from the Nile and Sunny South. If you know a good thing when you see it, this is the show for you." *(He shakes a finger at YOUNG HENRIETTA.)* "If you know a good thing when you see it…" These damn white boys and their "good things"… *(He becomes serious.)* What are you going to do?

YOUNG HENRIETTA: Well, I'm *not* going to put on a minstrel show.

FREDERICK: That's the spirit!

YOUNG HENRIETTA: *(She looks at the pile of manuscripts becoming more and more distraught and angry.)* Spirit's not going to pay my rent. Look at this…. Shakespeare… Dunbar… concert music… *(Suddenly, she shoves them all to the side.)* What I need is a miracle… a canon of tried-and-true Black classical plays. I need the library they burned in

Alexandria! I need dramas and comedies and operas and pageants, theatre that builds on archetypes of the great African warriors and queens. But what do I have? Little Egypt and Little Eva...! I'm praying for a miracle...

FREDERICK: When I was a slave, I prayed for my freedom for twenty years, but I didn't get an answer until I prayed with my legs.

YOUNG HENRIETTA: *(Looking at FREDERICK, she smiles.)* But you never told me what you're doing in Chicago... I hope you didn't come to see the "charming Creole ladies...?"

FREDERICK: *(Smiling.)* No, no... I'm here for the great world's fair.

YOUNG HENRIETTA: No, seriously.

FREDERICK: I am serious.

YOUNG HENRIETTA: No.

FREDERICK: Yes.

YOUNG HENRIETTA: I don't believe you.

FREDERICK: It's true.

YOUNG HENRIETTA: *(Confused.)* But the boycott... your pamphlet?

FREDERICK: Well... but I'm not here for the *American* exhibition. I'm here for Haiti...

YOUNG HENRIETTA: Haiti...?

FREDERICK: Yes, the Haitian government has invited me to come over and be part of their Pavilion… to give lectures on the only successful slave revolt in the world. Now, how could I turn down an opportunity to preach Black revolution in the great White City?

YOUNG HENRIETTA: *(Smiling.)* You couldn't.

FREDERICK: More than one way to shear a sheep. And speaking of sheep-shearing, I think I have a show for your theatre.

YOUNG HENRIETTA: Oh?

FREDERICK: Well, what if I told you I had in this satchel the manuscript of a play about the Haitian Revolution… a big, fat epic play in five acts—written by a Negro man whose mother actually came from Haiti… and that the whole thing is *in verse*?

YOUNG HENRIETTA: No!

FREDERICK: Yes.

HENRIETTA: *(A long pause.)* And you want *me* to produce it?

FREDERICK: I do.

YOUNG HENRIETTA: A play about slaves who kill off all the white people on their island?

FREDERICK: Well, there's a love story in there.

YOUNG HENRIETTA: Frederick Douglass, are you out of your mind?

FREDERICK: If I am, I've been that way for a long time and it seems to be working for me.

YOUNG HENRIETTA: A single Black woman... all by herself and brand-new in town, opening her first theatre with a play that advocates armed resistance...

FREDERICK: Well, I wouldn't say "advocates." *(Pause.)* "Glorifies." *(Nodding.)* It *glorifies* resistance.

YOUNG HENRIETTA: *Armed* resistance.

FREDERICK: *(Nodding thoughtfully.) Armed* resistance.

YOUNG HENRIETTA: No.

FREDERICK: Think about it.

YOUNG HENRIETTA: I just did.

FREDERICK: Well, think some more. *(He takes the manuscript out of the bag.)*

YOUNG HENRIETTA: You can leave that right there in your bag. I'm not going to read it.

FREDERICK: *(Exaggerating.)* Oh, Henrietta... it's *so* heavy. You're not going to make an old man haul this thing all over Chicago...?

YOUNG HENRIETTA: I can throw it out for you...

FREDERICK: Don't do that. *(He rises and thumps the manuscript down on her table.)* Burn it! Get some heat in this place… It's a damn barn! *(Suddenly a young woman appears at the door. MISS TAYLOR, 16, is deeply distraught. She wears the cheap, gaudy clothing of a chorine.)*

MISS TAYLOR: *(Out of breath.)* Miss Davis…? Are you Miss Davis? I have to talk to you…!

YOUNG HENRIETTA: *(Stiffly, to MISS TAYLOR.)* Excuse me…I have a guest.

MISS TAYLOR: Oh… *(Curtseying to FREDERICK.)* How do you do? *(Turning back to YOUNG HENRIETTA.)* Miss Davis, you have to help me… Please—

YOUNG HENRIETTA: This is Frederick Douglass…

MISS TAYLOR: What?

YOUNG HENRIETTA: Frederick Douglass.

MISS TAYLOR: Oh, my God… Mr. Douglass…!

FREDERICK: *(Nodding to her, and then turning back to YOUNG HENRIETTA.)* 'Til next we meet… And come see me at the Haitian Pavilion. *(Turning to MISS TAYLOR.)* You, too, Miss…?

MISS TAYLOR: Taylor.

FREDERICK: Miss Taylor. *(He nods to YOUNG HENRIETTA and exits, closing he door behind him.)*

MISS TAYLOR: Was that really Frederick Douglass?

YOUNG HENRIETTA: Yes. He's a friend of mine. I used to work for him.

MISS TAYLOR: Oh, Miss Davis, I'm so sorry. I don't mean to bother you, but I didn't know where else to go. I have to have a job. I haven't got any money, and he won't pay me my wages.

YOUNG HENRIETTA: Who won't pay you?

MISS TAYLOR: Mr. Jack. He said—

YOUNG HENRIETTA: Sam T. Jack?

MISS TAYLOR: Yes, he said—

YOUNG HENRIETTA: You're with *The Creole Show?*

MISS TAYLOR: I was, but I quit. Or maybe I was fired…

YOUNG HENRIETTA: You don't know?

MISS TAYLOR: Well, it was confusing. Mr. Jack asked me to do something, and he said he it was part of the show, but he says everything's part of the show… like his "rehearsals"… that's what he calls them… *(Embarrassed.)* So I just walked out, and when I went to collect my money, the manager said Mr. Jack told him not to pay me… And now I can't pay the rooming house—

YOUNG HENRIETTA: I don't need any dancers.

MISS TAYLOR: I can sing.

YOUNG HENRIETTA: A classical repertoire? *(Silence.)* I'm afraid I can't help you. I'm not producing any minstrel shows, *or* vaudeville, *or* burlesque…

MISS TAYLOR: I'll do anything. I can take care of the costumes or sell tickets, or sweep the floor. I can be your assistant. Just let me do anything—

YOUNG HENRIETTA: How old are you, Miss Taylor?

MISS TAYLOR: Twenty. *(Silence.)* Eighteen. *(Silence.)* Almost sixteen.

YOUNG HENRIETTA: Can you act?

MISS TAYLOR: Oh, yes, ma'am. When I was younger, I was Topsy in *Uncle Tom's*—

YOUNG HENRIETTA: *(Cutting her off.)* Read this for me… *(Handing her a script.)* It's Shakespeare…   In this scene Queen Cleopatra is explaining to her ladies what's going to happen to them if they surrender to the Romans… *(Pointedly.)* … how *they*—the African women—will be paraded through the streets and put on display, and how the Romans will ridicule them, and grope them, and treat them as if they are whores…   *(MISS TAYLOR holds the script for a long time, and then slowly she puts it down, tears welling up in her eyes. YOUNG HENRIETTA watches her.)*

MISS TAYLOR: *(Looking at the floor.)* I know what you think I am, Miss Davis. But I am a proud woman. I hired on with Mr. Jack in New York, because he said I wouldn't have to "black up" to play for white audiences… He said he wanted the audience to see us girls as we were—without blackface… to see how beautiful we were—you know—without—

YOUNG HENRIETTA: *(Cutting her off.)* Without your clothes. *(Long silence.)*

MISS TAYLOR: *(Looking up.)* You know he's got a bar over there attached to the theatre, and he makes us girls walk through that bar before the show… squeeze by all those men. And they're just waiting for us, too… *(YOUNG HENRIETTA nods.)* Please, Miss Davis. I have to— *(Suddenly there's a knock on the door.)*

YOUNG HENRIETTA: *(Holding up a hand.)* Yes? Who is it?

WILL: *(Offstage.)* William Cook.

YOUNG HENRIETTA: Come in, Mr. Cook. *(WILL COOK enters, his back to MISS TAYLOR. He is a young man, 24, very expensively dressed.)*

MISS TAYLOR: *(Confused.)* Should I leave?

YOUNG HENRIETTA: No, don't go. *(To WILL.)* Yes?

WILL: I'm looking for Miss Henrietta Vinton Davis?

YOUNG HENRIETTA: I'm she.

WILL: *(Bowing.)* Will Marion Cook.

YOUNG HENRIETTA: Mr. Cook, this is Miss Taylor. *(WILL turns to acknowledge MISS TAYLOR. He responds to her youth and her chorus-girl clothing.)*

WILL: Miss Taylor, it's a pleasure… *(Taking her hand, which she did not offer.)* A pleasure indeed… *(MISS TAYLOR looks nervously at YOUNG HENRIETTA.)*

YOUNG HENRIETTA: *(Coolly.)* And what can we do for you, Mr. Cook?

WILL: *(Releasing MISS TAYLOR's hand.)* Well, Miss Davis, I am a composer and I have a proposition for you—

YOUNG HENRIETTA: I don't do minstrel shows…

WILL: And I don't have any. I have written an opera, and I would like to propose that you co-produce it with me. I'm bringing in the principals, but I will be needing to cast the chorus here in Chicago… I have already retained Sissieretta Jones for the lead.

MISS TAYLOR: *(Breathless.)* Sissieretta Jones! Oh, Miss Davis, I heard her! She sang at the Grand Negro Jubilee at Madison Square Garden last year… ! There were eight thousand people—

WILL: *(Flirting with MISS TAYLOR.)* Well, just *two* months ago, she sang at Carnegie Hall, in a benefit for *my* opera…

YOUNG HENRIETTA: A Negro opera? *(He nods.)* A *Negro* opera…? *(Long silence.)* Oh, my god… This is the miracle… *(She starts laughing.)* This is the miracle! I can't believe it… Sissieretta Jones…? *(WILL looks at her confused. She is laughing.)* I *just* leased this theatre, and I have been tearing myself apart trying to figure out what kind of show I could open that could possibly compete with all this… all these… Ferris wheels and "Little Egypt…" Oh, my god.! … And here I was just lamenting the lack of a classical canon of Black drama…

WILL: Exactly! And it's high time we started to create that canon!

YOUNG HENRIETTA: Yes, it is! It is! *High* time! Mr. Cook, this is the best news I've heard in my life! What angel gave you the idea of writing a Black opera?

WILL: The angel of desperation, Miss Davis. I was playing the violin by the time I was four, and then I got into Oberlin before I was fifteen… and I raised the money to study in Germany… all the time thinking how I was going to conquer the world, and then I came back and—

YOUNG HENRIETTA: And nobody would give you a job.

WILL: Nobody would give me a job. Not even teaching. Nobody believes a Black man can play classical music.

YOUNG HENRIETTA: *(Nodding.)* And nobody believes that a Black woman can perform Shakespeare…

WILL: So, unless I want to give private lessons for the rest of my life, I am going to have to change people's minds.

YOUNG HENRIETTA: *(Nodding.)* Yes!

WILL: And so then I thought, "What can I write that will draw the most attention in the least amount of time…?" And then it hit me… an *opera*! *And* I am going to perform where the whole world is going to hear it!

YOUNG HENRIETTA: Where?

WILL: *(Exploding with pride.)* At the great World's Columbian Exposition! *(YOUNG HENRIETTA freezes.)* On August 25—Colored American Day at the fair!

YOUNG HENRIETTA: What about the boycott…?

WILL: We don't need it anymore! We won! They're giving us our own day at the fair!

YOUNG HENRIETTA: *(In disbelief.)* Our own *day…*

WILL: Exactly! *And* President Harrison himself wrote a letter on behalf of my opera, so now they *have* to let me do it. *(Turning to MISS TAYLOR.)* I met with the President.

MISS TAYLOR: The President…?

WILL: *(Chucking her under the chin.)* That's right, honey.

YOUNG HENRIETTA: *(Troubled.)* Mr. Cook, what is the name of your opera?

WILL: I'm calling it "Scenes from *Uncle Tom's Cabin.*" *(He turns back to MISS TAYLOR.)* Can you sing?

MISS TAYLOR: Oh… not opera…

WILL: *(Taking her hand.)* Well, that's okay, honey. We've got roles for a lot of folks in the crowd scenes… there's a slave auction, and a scene in the cotton fields … *(Stroking her arm.)* I'm sure I could find something for someone as pretty as you—

YOUNG HENRIETTA: Miss Taylor is here auditioning for me… *(Turning to MISS TAYLOR.)*

MISS TAYLOR: Yes, ma'am! *(She picks up the Shakespeare script.)*

YOUNG HENRIETTA: Oh, not the Shakespeare! Why don't you read something from this one? *(Grabbing the script that FREDERICK left, she hands it to MISS TAYLOR and turns to*

WILL.) I am afraid that I am not going to be able to help you after all. I just remembered that I have a prior commitment to... to... *(Reading the cover of the play.)* ... William Edgar Easton... to produce his play.

WILL: *(Confused.)* Easton...? I never heard of him. What's the play?

YOUNG HENRIETTA: What's the play...? *(Hastily reading the cover.) Dessalines...* Yes, *Dessalines.* It's about the slave revolt in Haiti. Very dramatic. Yes, very dramatic. We kill off all the white people. *(WILL is stunned. She acts puzzled by his reaction.)* In five acts... *(Another pause.)* In verse.

WILL: *(Stunned.)* You can't do that!

YOUNG HENRIETTA: *(Pretending not to understand.)* Oh, I certainly can... I've been directing verse drama for years... It's really no different from prose once you—

WILL: No... I mean—

YOUNG HENRIETTA: *(Cutting him off.)* And by a stroke of luck, the run is going to coincide with Colored American Day! Our own *day*!

MISS TAYLOR: Do you want me to read now?

YOUNG HENRIETTA: Oh, you found something? Yes, please. I'm sure that Mr. Cook would like to hear you as much as I.

MISS TAYLOR: This is Mr. Dessalines... *(She gives a spirited reading.)*

What will make ye masters here? Is his white tainted flesh invulnerable? Look upon us! I am as black as the shadows of night, with muscles of iron and a will that never was enslaved! What has he that I have not, save the arrogance of the accursed Caucasian blood? What hath these Franks that we are their household chattel—that we are their beasts? They suffer from the heat more than we, their sight is less keen, the evening dews hasten them to their graves and the noonday's sun finds them under cover. The very fibres of their frames are weak and puny—

YOUNG HENRIETTA: *(Cutting her off.)* Yes! Yes, Miss, Taylor, you're hired!

MISS TAYLOR: Oh, thank you, thank you! *(She hugs her. WILL starts to say something, but YOUNG HENRIETTA cuts him off.)*

YOUNG HENRIETTA: You know, Mr. Cook, your opera has got me thinking…   What if there was a *post*-bellum slave drama… you know…   one where we see the former slaves overthrowing their masters and then moving into the plantation…? We could call it "*Our* Old Kentucky Home…?" I might even write it myself… *(To MISS TAYLOR.)* What do you think? *(MISS TAYLOR is speechless. YOUNG HENRIETTA turns to WILL.)* I'll be in touch if I need any music… *(WILL, attempting in vain to catch MISS TAYLOR's eye, finally bows himself out. YOUNG HENRIETTA turns to MISS TAYLOR.)* Well, what are you standing around for? Go and get your things, Miss Taylor! We have work to do!

MISS TAYLOR: Yes, ma'am…yes, ma'am! *(She exits, as YOUNG HENRIETTA, shaking her head, picks up the script for* Dessalines.*)*

YOUNG HENRIETTA: Praying with my damn legs…

Blackout

End of Scene

Scene 7

Lights come up on the Liberty Hall dressing room. HENRIETTA still has the Liberian report in front of her.

ROBERT: *(A long silence. ROBERT gestures toward the paper.)* It's still there.

HENRIETTA: I see it.

ROBERT: Read it.

HENRIETTA: *(Ignoring him, she rises.)* Chicago taught me a lesson. It taught me that I have a choice… I can put on a show for the audience I *have*, or I can put on a show for the audience I *want* to have. Chicago taught me that if I don't choose the latter, it will be Zip Coon, Jim Crow, and "Creole ladies" for the rest of my life.

ROBERT: Henrietta… you made a promise. You made a promise to a dying man. And I am here to collect. *(He holds up the paper.)* March 16…

HENRIETTA: Robert—

ROBERT: March 16, 1924. Five months ago. I don't have the exact coordinates, but I don't believe it matters. We are somewhere in the middle of the ocean. Somewhere between Africa and Harlem. *(HENRIETTA shakes her head.)* We're in a cabin… a cabin on a ship—an ocean liner. It's a second-class cabin. Now, it's supposed to have been a first-class cabin. That is what was paid for, but it seems, at the last minute, there was some kind of a mix-up—the usual mix-up when a Black man wants first-class anything—and the only

46

cabins left are in second-class. There is a man in the bed. It's morning, but he is too sick to get up. In fact, he appears to be dying. Look... here he is... *(Indicating an area of the room.)* He's coughing. He can't get his breath. He's burning up with fever. Soaking the sheets with sweat. But he's not alone. There's a woman with him... one of his colleagues. She's talking to him. Do you remember what she says? *(Long pause.)*

HENRIETTA: *(She hesitates and then moves to a chair by the imaginary bed and begins to re-enact that night.)* "Robert, you listen to me. You're going to get well... In just a few days, we'll be landing in New York, and your wife and your brother are going to be there to meet us... And they're going to take you home... "

ROBERT: She promises.

HENRIETTA: *(Hesitating.)* "I promise."

ROBERT: And then the ship's doctor comes and he says he can't do anything. And you argue with him, don't you? You ask him to send for the captain.

HENRIETTA: Yes.

ROBERT: And you make another promise...

HENRIETTA: *(Re-enacting.)* "Robert, you listen to me. You're going to get well... and then after you're all healed up, you're going to come back to Africa... You're going to come on the Black Cross Line. You and Augusta are going to have yourselves a first-class cabin, with your own balcony."

ROBERT: And...?

HENRIETTA: *(Re-enacting.)* "And they'll seat you every night at the captain's table."

ROBERT: And...?

HENRIETTA: *(Looking at him evenly.)* "I promise."

ROBERT: But the man in the bed is not interested in the captain's table, is he? He knows he is dying. In fact, he knows he'll be dead by morning. His brain is on fire, but he is focused, Henrietta. What is he focused on? *(He holds up the paper.)* The Liberian report. *(She turns away.)* He's not thinking about himself, or his wife. He is thinking about the Liberian report! Why? Why, Henrietta, *why* is he thinking about that? *(Pause.)* Because he does not want to die in vain. He does not want any other Black person to die the way he will... to die on that miserable crossing, on a ship that is passing over the bones of millions—*millions* of Black bodies thrown off of white ships... And he knows they will throw him off in the morning. Oh, there will be a box and there will be some kind of words spoken... but it's all the same to this man. He knows that his body will be lost, lost in the middle of nowhere... no stone, no marker... sinking in that dark, swirling void that has swallowed his people's history and art... It's too late for him, but he can make sure that no one else will make this useless crossing. It's all here... *(Indicating the paper.)* It's all right here in his report... the truth. And with his dying breath, he delegates the woman in his second-class cabin to represent the mission, and he entrusts her to read and to deliver the report. *(He hands it to her.)* And then he asks her to promise that she will give it...

HENRIETTA: *(A long pause.)* "I promise."

ROBERT: And he dies. And the captain comes… but something happens between the time he dies and the arrival of the captain. What happens? *(HENRIETTA says nothing.)* What happens, Henrietta? *(He grabs her.)* What did you do? *(She turns away.)* You don't remember? Well, let's just see if we can figure out this mystery… Why don't we go down to the bottom of the ocean where that coffin has come to rest. Let's go down there and let's pry open that lid and take a look at what's in it.…

HENRIETTA: Robert—

ROBERT: Someone has dressed the sick man. He's wearing his finest suit… Jacket, and a fresh collar, striped tie… vest… Wait… There's something in his vest… but what is it? It's not a handkerchief, and it's not a watch… What is it, Henrietta? What did you put in his pocket? *(She turns away.)* Tell me! *What did you put in that dead man's pocket?*

HENRIETTA: *(Long silence.)* The Liberian report. *(He nods. HENRIETTA crosses to the door and then turns.)* Robert, you have a daughter.

ROBERT: No, I don't.

HENRIETTA: She was born a month ago…

ROBERT: No.

HENRIETTA: You know I'm telling the truth. It's my memory, my conscience animating you. You said so yourself… *(ROBERT is confused.)* Her name is "Roberta." *(Pause.)* After her daddy.

ROBERT: *(Thrown off.)* Augusta would have told me…

HENRIETTA: She didn't know she was pregnant until after we sailed, and her letters never caught up.

ROBERT: Why are you telling me this?

HENRIETTA: Because this is a conversation about your legacy. About the Liberian report.

ROBERT: It's a legacy of integrity. It's the legacy of a man who was willing to face the truth, even if it cost him his dreams.

HENRIETTA: … and his life.

ROBERT: And his life. I'm proud of that. You can tell her that.

HENRIETTA: I can't tell her anything, because she's as dead as you are. She didn't survive her crossing either. *(ROBERT sits.)* It was a hard pregnancy for Augusta. First you were gone, and then she found out you were dead. She was struggling with grief and fear about money… it was too much. Too much for her, and way too much for little Roberta.

ROBERT: Augusta…

HENRIETTA: Augusta will survive. She's a sculptor, an artist like me. She knows how to take her suffering and give it form, form that will bear witness to hope and beauty… form that will preserve life. A baby doesn't care about legacies. She only knows the hands that pick her up and the arms that hold her. She only knows the body that will feed her. She can't read. She can't even understand words. But she knows the sounds of her mother. She smells the smell of her body, she feels the warmth. That's a baby's truth. Presence. That's what has meaning. That's the only thing that has meaning: presence. And you didn't give her that. You didn't make the crossing back from your disillusionment. You didn't do whatever you had to do, you didn't tell yourself whatever you had to tell yourself, to keep your spirit alive for today and then the day after and the day after so that you could come back and be present for that child. Men have all these funny ideas about honor, and they usually involve dying or killing. We women can't afford notions about honor. We just worry about showing up, because that's the business of living. And if you are white, then you can look reality square in the face and keep going. But we have to pick and choose. We pick and choose what we can bear. We recognize a life-sustaining dream when we see one, and we grab it and we hold on for dear life. That's a skill. That's an achievement. And every single member of UNIA, every single follower of the Provisional President of Africa, Marcus Garvey, has earned the right to their dream. *(Pausing.)* I have a present for your daughter, Robert. She didn't live long enough for me to give it to her, but now that you're here, you can take it to her. *(HENRIETTA retrieves the paper that she put in her purse.)*

ROBERT: You never told me what it was…

HENRIETTA: You'll see… Manhattan. The Second Circuit Court of Appeals! *(Pause.)* A year ago.

Blackout

End of Scene

Scene 8

Lights come up in an antechamber in the courthouse for the United States Court of Appeals for the Second Circuit, lower Manhattan, May 1923. BENNY DANCY, a well-dressed older man, enters. He pours himself a glass of water from a pitcher and sits. HENRIETTA, in a simple suit, enters. BENNY rises.

BENNY: Lady Davis!

HENRIETTA: Mr. Dancy… Did you testify?

BENNY: Just finished.

HENRIETTA: How did it go?

BENNY: *(He sighs.)* Well, I think that it went about as well as it could, under the circumstances.

HENRIETTA: You didn't perjure yourself did you?

BENNY: No, Lady Davis, I did not. Have you been called yet?

HENRIETTA: Not yet… What did they ask you?

BENNY: That prosecutor, he handed me the empty envelope and he said, "Benny Dancy, do you recognize this?" And then, before I can answer, he goes and describes it to me, as if I couldn't see it for myself … He tells me it's got my name typed on it, and that in the corner is a rubber stamp of the Black Star Line. And I look at it, and I say, "Yes, sir." And then he says, "Do you know what was in it?" And I say, "No, sir." But he's not happy with that, so he asks me again if I can identify anything that was in it, and I say, "No, sir." So then he says my name, in case that's the problem: "Benny Dancy… can you tell us what was in it?" And I say, "No, sir." And this is not perjury, Lady Davis, because that envelope has been all over the offices of the Federal Bureau of Investigation, and I don't know what those white people have put in it or taken out of it. I sweep the floors at Pennsylvania Station, and I have been doing that job for thirteen years … and I can testify that white people, when they think nobody is looking, will do things that you can't even believe. I mean, anything you can think of, they have done it and I have cleaned up after it. Trust me. So I was telling the truth when I said I did not know what had been in that envelope. *(HENRIETTA laughs.)* So now the man shows me some pamphlets for the Black Star Line and he says, "Can you identify any of these?" and I say, "No, sir," because I don't know where he got them or who they were sent to… *(Pause.)* But he goes ahead and enters that envelope as evidence.

HENRIETTA: *(Smiling.)* You know, Mr. Dancy, you are the key witness for the prosecution.

BENNY: Well, they're not getting anything out of me. I don't see how they can convict Mr. Garvey of mail fraud on the evidence of one empty envelope, when nobody even knows what was in it.

HENRIETTA: They don't need evidence to convict when a Black man's in the dock.

BENNY: Well, that's a fact. But Mr. Garvey, he should know that we are all behind him.

HENRIETTA: *(A pause.)* How many shares of the Black Star Line *do* you own?

BENNY: Fifty-three. Fifty-three shares.

HENRIETTA: Two hundred and sixty-five dollars…

BENNY: Yes, ma'am. And I keep the certificates all in an album for my children.

HENRIETTA: Did you know that the Black Star Line has been dissolved? We went bankrupt earlier this year.

BENNY: Yes, ma'am I know that.

HENRIETTA: I'm afraid your certificates are worthless now.

BENNY: Well, with all due respect, that's where I have to disagree with you, Lady Davis.

HENRIETTA: Oh…?

BENNY: I told you I work at Penn Station. And, when I'm working, people there, they act like they don't even see me. They just walk right by me—right *into* me sometimes… on their way to the trains. Drop their cigarettes and their trash right in front of me, like I wasn't even there. And my supervisor calls me "boy." Half my age, but he calls me "boy." The only time they see me is if they have a question about where their platform is or what time their train leaves. They're all in a big hurry to get somewhere. They treat me like a janitor. They don't know I'm a stockholder. They don't know that I've been saving up money from my paychecks week after week, and that I have been buying up stock certificates. They don't know I own fifty-three shares in the world's first Black steamship company. I see them with their fancy suits and their briefcases and their fur coats and their carts full of luggage. I see them rushing to catch their trains… Lady Davis, they are not going anywhere… not anywhere it all, because all those trains can do is take them some other place that is run by white people. It's going to be the same. Wherever they go, it's going to be the same… But I own something that can take people somewhere—across a whole ocean, to a place that's not run by white people, a place they can't even imagine.

Those stock certificates that you tell me are worthless… Well, Lady Davis, I know you know what they look like. They have a picture on the front. A picture of a globe with Africa at the center. *That*, right there, if a man knows what to do with it, is worth his five dollars. Right there. And it *says* it, right there, "*Africa: The Land of Opportunity.*" And every time I look at those certificates, I feel the floor under my feet move—just a little, like I was on the deck of a ship… just a little rocking motion… And I catch a smell of salt air and fertile ground, and I hear the call of home, of Africa… the call of freedom. When I look at those certificates, I am underway. I don't care if that Black Star Line is bankrupt or not. That's got nothing to do with my stock certificates. The Bible says "Faith is the substance of things hoped for," and I never understood what that meant. How can a thing you hope for have any substance? But the day I held that first stock certificate in my hand, I understood. Lady Davis, I am a man of substance today because I own fifty-three shares of the Black Star Line.

Blackout

End of Scene

Scene 9

Lights come up on the Liberty Hall dressing room. ROBERT is holding the paper that HENRIETTA has handed him. He unfolds it and nods.

ROBERT: Ten shares of the Black Star Line… *(HENRIETTA nods.)* Signed by Marcus Garvey.

HENRIETTA: For the spirit of your daughter.

ROBERT: *(Rising.)* I'll be leaving now. *(He picks up his Liberian report and puts it back in his pocket. He hands HENRIETTA the notes for her speech.)* Don't forget your speech… Not that a woman like you would really need her notes... *(ROBERT opens the door and steps out into a brilliant light. As he closes the door, the lighting in the room returns to normal. HENRIETTA collects her notes.)*

HENRIETTA: *(Crossing to the mirror, she speaks with clarity and conviction .)* "I esteem it a very great honor to have the pleasure of introducing to you the man of the hour…The man who has stood upon the Olympian heights, who has caught the vision of the gods for his people, whose clarion voice has been echoed from mountaintop to mountaintop until it has circled the globe, calling his brothers to arms. That man is the undaunted, the unconquerable, the incomparable *Marcus Garvey*..."

Blackout

End of Play

Easter Sunday

A One-Act Play

Cast of Characters

DEL: A lesbian butch, 40. Working-class, Italian American background.

FLORA: A lesbian fem, 33. Working-class, also Italian American. Del's partner.

MARTY: A lesbian butch, 56. Upper-middle-class.

Scene

A bench in Morningside Park, the stoop outside a Greenwich Village walk-up, and the interior living room of the walk-up.

Time

Morning, April 10, 1960.

Easter Sunday

Scene 1

A bench in Morningside Park, around noon on April 10, 1960. The sunlight is brilliant and saturates the stage. FLORA, 33, sits on a bench. FLORA is "high femme," but she punches well above her weight. She wears a floral chiffon dress with a full skirt, a cardigan sweater draped over her shoulders, and a floral "half-hat" pinned over her curls. She wears a corsage and carries a small purse. It's Easter Sunday, and this is her best outfit. DEL enters carrying two snow cones. DEL, 40, wears a men's short jacket with a zipper and slacks. Her short, dark hair is slicked back in a ducktail. DEL is deeply religious and that religion is FLORA.

DEL: Here, baby… Snow cone for my girl. *(Handing it to her.)*

FLORA: Del! First a corsage, and now a snow cone! What do you think this is?

DEL: What do I think it is? It's Easter Sunday! *(Looking at her.)* Hey, this was your idea, not mine …

FLORA: No… All I said was that I wanted to go to the Easter service at the Cathedral. *(Eating.)* That's all I said. Nothing about flowers or snow cones. You… me… St. John the Divine. *(Eating.)* That's all I said.

DEL: Well, what's Easter without the flowers, and what's Morningside Park without a snow cone?

59

FLORA: *(Looking around, she gives DEL a quick kiss.)*
What's any of it without you, baby? *(DEL looks at her for a
moment, and then grabs her and kisses her back. FLORA,
nervous, pulls away.)* Hey…

DEL: What…? You started it…

FLORA: Yeah, well *I* wasn't puttin' on a show.

DEL: Nobody was lookin'…

FLORA: That was the most beautiful Easter service I ever
been to… and I been to a few.

DEL: *(Exaggerating her response.)* Tell me about it… *Every*
Easter. *Every* effin' Easter. Never any *other* Sunday, oh no…
but *Easter—*

FLORA: *(Defensive.)* Hey, a lot of people just go on Easter!

DEL: I'm not judgin'…

FLORA: That music… You gotta admit—that music…
(Singing.) "Welcome happy morning…" I don't know why…
I love that hymn…! *(She jumps up, singing.) "Welcome, happy
morning!" (Louder, twirling.) "Welcome, happy morning,"*
everybody—!

DEL: *Now* who's puttin' on a show? *(FLORA keeps twirling.)*
Better watch out… *(FLORA twirls.)* They'll come and cart
you off to Bellvue…

FLORA: I'm so happy today…! Everything is so beautiful!
The sky, the grass, the park… and that *service*…! Wasn't it
beautiful? *(DEL looks at her.)* Come on, Del… wasn't it?

DEL: It was *church.*

FLORA: Yeah, I know, but the big arches, and the choir, and the chimes, and—

DEL: And the hypocrites and the bigots.

FLORA: Well, I didn't notice any.

DEL: Baby, that's because you don't look like me.

FLORA: *(Sitting down, serious.)* Thanks for comin' with me. I know you didn't want to.

DEL: *(Shrugging.)* Whatever blows your skirt up.

FLORA: *(Swatting her.)* Del!

DEL: What?

FLORA: Hey, I haven't been inside that cathedral since I was sixteen years old and livin' in the Bronx.

DEL: The damn thing was always under construction when I was a kid. I'd ride my bicycle past it... Traffic was always gettin' blocked up.

FLORA: Yeah... that's how come my mother made us go. She read in the paper that they finally finished it, and they were going to open it—the whole thing, not just part of it, but the whole thing—for the first time in a hundred years. She told my dad she always wanted to know what it looked like. *(Pausing.)* I remember she made us get all dressed up, and she bought one of those new floppy hats... big as an umbrella... It was right after Thanksgiving. Must have been the last time all of us were together, because a week after that, they bombed Pearl Harbor, and then everything changed. *(FLORA gets quiet. DEL watches her.)*

DEL: Yeah… Everything sure changed.

FLORA: How old were you?

DEL: When the war broke out? Twenty-one. Twenty-one and goin' crazy. My brothers and the guys in the shop all went out and joined up, leavin' me just sittin' on my hands.

FLORA: My dad joined up, too… I think he was looking for an excuse to leave. He and Ma had a big fight before he shipped out. She was terrified of being alone… I think she knew that if he left, he was never coming back… even if he wasn't killed.

DEL: *(Lost in her own thoughts, she shakes her head.)* Thank God for the WACs.

FLORA: *(In her own memories, nodding.) Everything changed…*

DEL: *(Remembering.)* Man, when I heard they were starting a women's army corps, I couldn't wait. I must have been the first one through the door.

FLORA: Ma went back to work, and I got a job after school.

DEL: All those women… *nothing* but women… Flora, you never saw so many women in one place without men. Fort Des Moines was like a whole village of women. *(Nudging her.)* You woulda loved it.

FLORA: What? Are you kidding? I would have been scared to death!

DEL: No…

FLORA: Oh, yeah!

DEL: Really?

FLORA: When I was at Hunter, they leased out part of the school for the women's navy auxiliary… It was a big training center for the WAVES. Those girls were all over the place… in the dormitories and in the dining halls. They were sending in two thousand new ones every week!

DEL: *(Nudging her.)* Musta had to work fast.

FLORA: *(Shaking her head.)* They scared me to death.

DEL: Why?

FLORA: Because they all wore these uniforms, and they marched around in formations, and they weren't just from New York. I mean, they were coming in from Florida, and Texas, and all over the place… all by themselves—a million miles from their families and their boyfriends. And they didn't know where they were going, and they didn't care! They were playing records and smuggling in booze, and dancing with each other—like it was one big adventure! And here was mousy, little me, still living at home with Ma, scared of my own shadow… thinking it was some kind of big expedition just taking the subway by myself to the Bronx!

DEL: Well, you're one of us now, baby. *(FLORA blushes.)* What changed your mind? *(FLORA shakes her head.)* Come on… Something must have happened…? When I met you, you were already one of the regulars at the Sea Colony. *(FLORA shakes her head.)* Tell me… what was it? *(Tugging on her sleeve.)* C'mon.

FLORA: *(Suddenly serious.)* No, Del… Quit… Don't spoil the morning.

DEL: *(Shaken by her seriousness.)* Oh, baby, you know I wouldn't do that. *(Silence.)* Want another snow cone? Hmm? *(DEL sings, trying to make her laugh.)* "Welcome, happy morning…" *(FLORA swats her, still upset.)* You know, I kinda dig this Easter thing.

FLORA: No, you don't. You hate church.

DEL: I hate church, but I dig the Resurrection. *(FLORA looks skeptically at her.)* And you don't believe me, but I do. See, I rose from the dead. *(FLORA shakes her head.)* I did. When I got sober… *(She takes FLORA's hand.)* See, I had this girlfriend in the WACS… Shirley. *(FLORA, nervous in public, pulls her hand away.)* I told you I had a girlfriend, right? I was really in love. Yeah. First time. But after the war, she wanted to stay in, and I wanted to get back home to New York… Shirley was a mechanic. They trained her. She didn't think she'd ever get a job outside the military, being a girl, and Black and all… Probably right, but I took it all personal… I left and she stayed, and then she went overseas, and I started drinking… not too much at first, but every night. Every night… and then I started drinkin' more and earlier… and I couldn't stop. But then one night… it was 1952, and I see this angel walk in the bar. *(FLORA rolls her eyes.)* No, listen… And nobody else knew she was an angel, not even her… but *I* knew. I knew that she had been sent there just for me. I knew this was my last chance, and that if I blew it, I would never see her again. Yeah, so I stopped drinking and I got sober. And it's a damn good thing I did, because if I hadn't stopped, she wouldn't have had nobody to buy her snow cones on Easter and take her to St. John the Divine…

FLORA: *(She punches DEL's arm and rises.)* Come on…

DEL: What? Jesus the only one allowed to resurrect?

FLORA: *(Punching DEL again.)* Don't be sacrilegious…

DEL: Oh, and now she's Rocky Graziano… Okay… you wanna go, let's go… *(Playfully DEL puts up her fists. Ignoring her, FLORA opens her purse, takes out a compact, and begins to fix her lipstick. Still seated, DEL watches her.)* So, babe, I gotta ask you a favor. *(Long silence.)* I said, I gotta ask you for a favor.

FLORA: *(Still looking in the mirror.)* So ask.

DEL: *(Nervous, she rises.)* Well, I wanna stop somewhere on the way back to the apartment.

FLORA: It's a free country.

DEL: I want you to go with me.

FLORA: Where?

DEL: Well, it's a place on West 9th Avenue.

FLORA: Yeah… You know somebody there?

DEL: Yeah... Sort of…

FLORA: Why do you want me to go?

DEL: I want she should meet you.

FLORA: Why? *(Long silence.)* Del…?

DEL: Look, baby, I came to church with you… You can do me a favor.

FLORA: Del…? What's going on?

DEL: It's a surprise, okay. It's a surprise. You gonna come or not?

FLORA: Well, I'd like to know who it is…

DEL: Well, then it wouldn't be a surprise, would it?

FLORA: Del—

DEL: C'mon, baby… Let's agitate the gravel!

FLORA: *(Turning and staring.)* "Agitate the gravel?"

DEL: Just something the kids say.

FLORA: *(Imitating DEL.)* "Agitate the gravel…" *(She bursts out laughing. She enjoys busting DEL when she's trying to act cool.)*

DEL: *(Embarrassed, she tugs FLORA's skirt.)* C'mon. Let's go.

FLORA: *(Still teasing.)* "Agitate the gravel!" *(They exit, FLORA laughing.)*

Blackout

End of Scene

Scene 2

Lights come up on the front stoop of a four-story, brownstone, walk-up apartment building in Greenwich Village, same morning. Dark, angular shadows from the buildings cut across the sunlit street. DEL and FLORA are just arriving.

FLORA: *(Anxious, but attempting to laugh it off.)* This is the place? Brownstone… Fancy-schmanzy.

DEL: Yeah. *(DEL reaches over to push the buzzer. FLORA stops her.)*

FLORA: Del! You gotta tell me who this is…

DEL: I'll introduce you.

FLORA: *(Getting panicky.)* No! Tell me now!

DEL: You'll recognize her…

FLORA: Tell me now, or I'm leaving. *(A standoff. She turns to make good on her threat.)*

DEL: Okay, okay… Wait… Flora, come back. *(FLORA stands on the street.)* It's Mrs. Mann.

FLORA: "Mrs. Mann…?" I don't know who that is.

DEL: Yeah, you do… From Cherry Grove… Fire Island…? *(FLORA gives her a warning look.)* Her place was next door to the cottage we always rent… We'd see her every summer… on the boardwalks…

FLORA: *(Warning.)* Del…

DEL: *(Forging ahead.)* Big gal... kinda butchy... *(FLORA looks confused.)* Yeah... She and her girfriend had those dogs... the funny little ones with the stumpy legs...

FLORA: The corgis...?

DEL: Yeah. Mrs. Mann and her girlfriend were always out walkin' the corgis. *(FLORA's expression has become very grim.)* Yeah... you remember... and they used to put those little bows on the dogs...

FLORA: *(Shaking her head. This is not about dogs.)* No!

DEL: *(Playing dumb.)* Yeah, sure... They used to tie a blue bow around the neck of the boy dog, and then they stuck a pink bow on top of the girl dog... They'd make a joke out of it. They would say they did it 'cuz they got tired of people all the time askin,' "Which one is the boy?" *(FLORA has started walking again.)* What...? You thought it was funny!

FLORA: Well, this isn't.

DEL: Listen, Flora—

FLORA: No. I'm not going to listen. Del, this is about buying the cottage. *(DEL doesn't say anything. FLORA raises her voice.)* This is about buying that damn cottage! Tell me it isn't! *(DEL doesn't say anything.)* I knew it! I knew it! *(She starts walking again. DEL chases after her.)*

DEL: Flora, wait! Wait! *(DEL tries to block her. FLORA won't let her touch her.)* Okay... it's about the cottage... What's the crime? Buyin' a little dream house? Tryin' to do a little something nice for the woman I love? What's so terrible about that... hunh? Get my girl a little summer place down by the ocean where she doesn't have to be so nervous all the time about what people think... Where's the crime?

FLORA: You know.

DEL: *(Getting annoyed.)* No, I don't.

FLORA: The owner said no.

DEL: Yeah. A lotta people say no. You said no.

FLORA: You were a drunk!

DEL: Well, I changed. People can change, you know. Maybe the owner is going to change… or… maybe… *maybe* we do a little something to *help* her change... like gettin' one of her neighbors… *(Pointing her thumb toward the Mann apartment for emphasis.) ... gettin' one of her neighbors* who is *also* in the Cherry Grove Property Owners Association, to recommend that she sell to us….

FLORA: No!

DEL: Mrs. Mann and her girlfriend… they live right next door to the cottage that's for sale. So… what if she says she's met us, and she likes us, and that it would be a great idea for her friend to sell her cottage to us…? Just ask her to put in a good word… Baby, that's all I'm tryin' to do here—

FLORA: *(Deeply upset.)* People like that don't change. They *never* change.

DEL: *(Concerned.)* Baby…

FLORA: *(Pushing her away.)* No, Del! They *don't!* I *told* you to leave it alone! I *told* you! *(DEL reaches for her.)* Leave me alone. *(DEL backs off quickly and sits on the stoop.)* Come on… let's go home. *(DEL doesn't budge.)* What?

DEL: You've been upset about something ever since Morningside Park. Now, I'm not leavin' here until you tell me what it is.

FLORA: *(Defensive.)* I was *happy* in Morningside Park… I was singin.'

DEL: When you were talkin' about all those Navy girls in your dormitories… and how you were scared of them, and I asked you what changed… *(Long silence.)*

FLORA: Come on, Del. Don't spoil the day.

DEL: Nope.

FLORA: Don't do this. *(A standoff.)*

DEL: *(Breaking the silence, she jumps up.)* Hey! Talkin' about the war… did I ever tell you about the time I integrated the service club at Ft. Des Moines?

FLORA: Del…

DEL: You know how I did it? *(FLORA doesn't respond.)* Like this, baby. Just like this. *(She slams herself down on the stoop.)* Just sittin' my ass down and not gettin' up. *(FLORA doesn't say anything.)* Yeah, and my girlfriend didn't like me doin' that any more than you like me sittin' here now. But I did it anyway. See, Shirley was Black, and on the base, they had a separate service club for the Blacks. Yeah… see, the Chinese girls and the Puerto Rican girls and the Indian girls… *they* could all go to the service club for us white girls. But the Blacks weren't allowed. They had to have their own club. Didn't make any sense to anybody. Especially not to me, because there was nowhere in Iowa I could go have a beer with my girl. So me and some of my pals just "dropped in" one day at Shirley's club. Walked in and sat down. And

Shirley thought I was gonna get us both kicked out of the WAC's. But that was the end of it. That club was completely desegregated from that day on. *(Pause.)* Sometimes all it takes, baby, is somebody just sittin' down and not gettin' up. *(She pats the stoop next to her, inviting FLORA.)*

FLORA: *(A long pause. She becomes more and more agitated as she speaks.)* Okay, Del. You wanna ruin Easter…? Okay. I was at Hunter College… Hunter *in the Bronx—not* the one on Park Avenue. Yeah, that's an important part of the story… I was livin' at home, takin' a bus… working… and goin' to school to be a nurse. And I guess the plan was, I was goin' to take care of Ma until Daddy came home… *(She stops. DEL, still seated, reaches toward her, but FLORA steps back.)* So, I had this teacher. *(She stops again.)* Yeah, he was a teacher all right. *(She stops again.)* Del, I can't talk about this.

DEL: Okay.

FLORA: Can we go?

DEL: Baby, I'm stayin' right here. I told you. *(Another long pause. Angry, FLORA continues.)*

FLORA: So he's a doctor… you know… a doctor teachin' anatomy to the nursing students. And he starts askin' me out. I'm still a kid. Seventeen. So he comes over and meets Ma, and she goes ape over him… And he's takin' me to the movies and he's takin' me dancin'. And Ma… she's tellin' everybody how her daughter's goin' with a *doctor.* She's warnin' me all the time to play my cards right, so things will "work out." And I don't know what cards she's talkin' about, so she tells me not to make myself "disagreeable." *(DEL, sensing what's coming, stands up abruptly.)* See, you don't want to hear this… *(DEL sits down again.)*

DEL: I do. *(Pause.)* I do. *(Pause.)* Baby, I do.

FLORA: *(A long breath. She is very, very angry.)* So while I'm all busy tryin' not to be disagreeable, I end up bein' pregnant. *(Long pause. She looks at Del as if to dare her to get up. DEL, with great effort, stays seated.)* Yeah. *(Another very long pause.)* And I don't know what to do, you know… 'cause I'm *seventeen*… so I tell Ma. And she tells me not to do anything. She says not to tell the doctor, because he's gonna want to make me… you know—get rid of it. She says I gotta wait. So I wait. I wait a month and then another month and then another month and I'm not sayin' anything, but I am growing a baby inside me, Del. I mean, there are definitely two of us. I can feel it. And all this time, he's takin' me sailin' with his friends, and we're havin' parties at his club, and he's drivin' me out to Montauk in his car. And Ma keeps tellin' me to play my cards right… play my cards right… But I guess I must have played the wrong one, because he finally figures out I'm pregnant, and it's too late—you know… so he says it's not his, and that I been sleepin' with other guys, and he puts on this big show of bein' mad at me… and he says I'm tryin' to trap him… and then all his friends won't have anything to do with me… and I drop outta college on account of the way they're all talkin' about me. And Ma's—she's tellin' me it's all my fault. Like I did something awful to her, too. *(FLORA stops. Long pause. DEL rises and takes a step toward her. FLORA takes a step back.)* I had a baby, Del. *(DEL nods.)* I had a beautiful, little baby girl. And I gave her away, because that's what Ma told me I had to do. Because I hadn't played my cards right. *(Pause.)* Del, I gave away my baby. My own baby. *(DEL puts her arm around her waist.)* And the day after I did it, I knew it was the worst thing I had ever done—the worst thing I could ever do, because I wanted that baby and I let her talk me into giving her up. *(DEL tries to hug her, but FLORA holds her off.)* Don't look at me like that, Del! I did it. I signed those papers. I took my hand, my own hand… *(She holds up her hand, angry with herself.)* … and I signed them. And I was eighteen by then. I wasn't a kid. I did it. *(Pause.)* But it was the last time I ever let anybody tell me what to do. I moved right out and I got a job in the Village, and I got a room in a building with a lot of single girls… and that suited me fine, because I'd had enough of men. And then I found out most of the girls were lesbian. And not one of them *ever* let *anybody* tell them what to do, and that's when I realized that was what I wanted to be. One of them.

DEL: Well, you sure are… One of *us*.

FLORA: I'm never going to be agreeable again.

DEL: Suits me. *(DEL sits.)*

FLORA: So *now* can we go? *(DEL doesn't move.)* The woman who owns that cottage is *not* gonna sell to us. She and your "Mrs. Mann" are never gonna let us join their little club. Oh, and, by the way, you and Shirley integrated the *Black women's* service club. Don't think for a second they were gonna let you integrate the *white women's* club… because those country club types are never going to change! They don't even want their own babies if… if… when… *(FLORA runs abruptly out of words.)*

DEL: Hey, hey, hey! Marty's not like that.

FLORA: *(Whipping around.)* "*Marty*…?"

DEL: *(Jerking her thumb toward the door.)* Mrs. Mann. Marty Mann.

FLORA: *(Eyebrows flying up.)* "Marty?" *You slept with her?*

DEL: No!

FLORA: Then what's with the "Marty?"

DEL: I know her from Alcoholics Anonymous. She started the meetings in Cherry Grove.

FLORA: Not very anonymous.

DEL: It's okay. She doesn't care.

FLORA: Yeah, I'll bet…

DEL: No, listen… Marty—Mrs. Mann—is this big spokesman for the National Council on Alcoholism. She flies all over the world and gives speeches, tellin' her story. She was one of the first women in AA. *(FLORA looks skeptical.)* Baby, she's been on the television. It's not a big secret. She's not one of those phoneys like you're talkin' about. She's different. She's one of us.

FLORA: "One of us!" *(Shaking her head.)* You know what her little Cherry Grove crowd calls us renters? "Toughies" and "greasers" and "bull dykes!" That's what they call people like us.

DEL: *(Jumping in, agitated.)* No! That's what they call people like *me*. It's me—*me!*— they don't want! The duck's ass, and the chinos, and the motorcycle boots… They look at you and they see the dress and heels—okay, maybe not from Saks— but still *respectable*. This… *(Indicating herself.)* … *this* is *not* respectable. And you only get dragged into it, when they see you walkin' next to me. *(Going over the edge now.)* And don't you think it *kills* me to see you getting' disrespected on account of me? *(FLORA tries to interrupt.)* No, Flora. This is *my* turn. This is why I'm sittin' on this damn stoop on Easter morning. You remember that book *Well of Loneliness*…? Yeah, I know… kinda cheeseball, but that part where Stephen is pushin' her girlfriend away—pushin' away the woman she loves—tellin' her how she doesn't love her , tellin' her to go be with some man… I get that. I do. I *live* it. It *kills* me to see how people look at you when they figure out you're my girl. I can't go by the school where you work without gettin' you fired, and you know that. You know it, Flor. You know I'm talking straight now. But, see, I got some options that Stephen didn't have thirty years ago, because now there's this island, this village... this village on an island that's all filled with people like us. I can buy you a cottage on that island, Flora. I can buy it and put it in your name, and you can be a member of the Cherry Grove Homeowners Association. You won't have to be a renter or a day-tripper anymore. You'll be a *homeowner*, and nobody can ever evict you, or refuse to rent to you, again. You can spend the whole damn summer out there, if you want to... Queen of your own island. Baby, I wanna give you that... *(Pause.)* I owe it to you.

FLORA: Del... *(She turns away, shaking her head.)* You don't get it.

DEL: What? *(Pause.)* What don't I get?

FLORA: *(Turning to face her.)* All that stuff you want to protect me from... *that stuff* is why I'm with you. *(DEL looks confused.)*
That's why I love you! You've never been anybody but yourself! You've never worn a dress, and you never had a boyfriend, and no matter how people treat you, you never change to please them. You never went off and tried to be somebody you weren't. You never went off and got yourself pregnant doin' something you hated, and then let someone talk you into bein' ashamed and giving up the thing you love the most, just because of what people might think. You're strong, and you're brave, and you're the most honest person I ever met... and I feel like I'm the luckiest girl when I'm with you. And when people treat us like dirt, I just think how it's makin' me get a little bit more like you. And that's the greatest thing in the world—to be like you. *(DEL is speechless. FLORA looks away.)*

DEL: *(After a moment.)* Flora… Look at me, baby. I don't know that I'm all those things you think I am, but I do know that one conversation on Easter morning isn't going to change who I am. *(Pause.)* Do you think it will? *(Pause.)* Do you really think that me talkin' to this woman is going to turn me into a pumpkin?

FLORA: I don't know, Del. But we're happy. We were havin' a happy mornin' and then your wantin' to be in their club—

DEL: Baby, I just want to buy you a house. *(Silence.)* That's it. *(Pause.)* Honest. *(Pause. DEL crosses cautiously to the door and rings the bell. Pause.)* It's different in AA… There's a bond… Like we all have this disease, and it's tryin' to kill all of us… the millionaires and the skid row bums, the men, the women, the gays, the straights… it doesn't care. It's tryin' to kill us all. And we're there tryin' to save each other. It's not like anything I ever felt, even in the WACs. And that's why I know I can ask Marty *(FLORA reacts.)*—and she's "Marty" because we all call each other by our first names… I can ask *Marty* to sponsor us as homeowners. Because she knows I'm sober and she knows we're gonna be good neighbors… because of the AA thing.

FLORA: But that's not what those people care about! You think that country club set never gets drunk and fights and cheats and steals? Because I *know* they do. And they'd rather have some loudmouth millionaire next door who has screaming fights every night with her drunk debutante girlfriend than a boring old greaser couple like us. You just don't get it… *(Stubbornly, DEL rings the bell again.)* Del, listen to me! It's not about manners! We're never going to be good enough! *(Suddenly the door swings open. MARTY, 56, wearing an expensive but disheveled bathrobe and badly hungover, lurches into the doorway. She is a large and tall woman, and she knows how to use her size to intimidate. Shielding her face from the light, she looks like hell.)*

MARTY: What the hell do you want, ringing my doorbell ten times on a Sunday fucking morning? *(FLORA and DEL are both speechless.)*

FLORA: *(After a moment.)* We're sorry… there's been a mistake… *(She turns to go.)*

DEL: *(Stepping up and overriding.)* Mrs. Mann? Mrs. Marty Mann…?

MARTY: *(Squinting.)* Do I know you…?

DEL: Sort of—

FLORA: Come on, Del…

DEL: *(Introducing.)* Del Vitale and Florence De Rosa. We were your next-door neighbors last summer… in Cherry Grove…? *(A long pause.)*

MARTY: *(Chilly.)* I have no idea what you are talking about.

FLORA: Come *on*, Del! *(Pulling Del's arm as she steps away from the door.)* Let's go. *(To MARTY.)* This is a *mistake*.

DEL: *(Getting fired up, she shakes off FLORA's arm and confronts MARTY.)* No! It's no mistake. You and your partner own the cottage just south of the ferry… the pink one, and you got two corgis—with the bows—

MARTY: Mrs. Mann is not here. *(A stunned silence.)*

DEL: *(Recovering, she crosses her arms. A showdown.)* We'll wait.

FLORA: Del!

MARTY: I'm afraid there's no point in waiting. You see, she's dead.

FLORA: Thank you. We're sorry—

DEL: No, we're not sorry. I don't believe you.

MARTY: Well, you should, because I killed her. *(She turns and slams the door on them. After a moment of stunned silence, FLORA turns and stares at DEL.)*

DEL: *(Focused on the door.)* I'm not leavin.'

FLORA: Del, she's drunk! Easter mornin' and she's drunk!

DEL: Yeah, and that's why I'm not leavin'.

FLORA: She *doesn't* want to talk to you!

DEL: You go on home, babe. I'm gonna stay here.

FLORA: Del!

DEL: You don't understand how it works... We don't walk away from each other like that. That's what sponsorship's all about. That's why we all have one. We save each other... There's women I've sponsored that I had to go haul out of the bars... One of them even slugged me.

FLORA: That's disgusting. She's disgusting.

DEL: It's a disease, baby, and I have it. Don't talk like that.

FLORA: You're different.

DEL: I'm sober, baby, and that's the only difference.

FLORA: Well, you're not her sponsor and the only reason you want to stay is to see if you can get in her club. *(Escalating.)* You're just like my mother… Just rub elbows with them one time, just catch a whiff of that money… and suddenly you just gotta get in that club… do anything to get in that club…

DEL: Flor…

FLORA: No, see… we're fighting already! She's got us fighting already! She ruined our Easter before you even rang the doorbell she ruined our morning! They're like that, Del… They ruin everything they touch! They broke my mother and me apart, and now they're doing it to us… *(Becoming hysterical.)* They'll ruin everything… everything that's real and innocent… They just take and take and take. Even when they're giving, they're still taking! They ruin everything… Come on, Del… let's go!

DEL: *(Shaking her head sadly.)* I can't.

FLORA: *(Enraged, she turns to go, screaming her words out in anger.) Well, you just be sure you play your cards right! (She exits running.)*

DEL: *(Calling after her.)* Flora…! *(DEL sighs and approaches the door again. With deliberation, she rings the bell and waits. She pushes the bell again. Suddenly the door flies open.)*

MARTY: I told you she's dead! *(MARTY attempts to close the door, but DEL has got her foot in it.)*

DEL: I'm a friend of Bill W…

MARTY: I don't give a crap who you're a friend of. She's still dead.

DEL: Well, then, I'd like to see the body.

MARTY: *(Sizing her up.)* Oh, you would, would you?

DEL: Yeah. *(Suddenly MARTY opens her robe seductively, revealing an expensive slip, half falling off. She loses her balance, the robe slips down, and she falls in the doorway. DEL pushes her way past her into the hall.)* Okay, buddy… that's it… I'm comin' in. *(She hauls MARTY over the threshold none too gently and kicks the door shut.)*

Blackout

End of Scene

Scene 3

Lights come up on the interior of MARTY's apartment. It is a very modern, Greenwich Village, upper-middle-class apartment. The apartment has tall windows with floor-to-ceiling-curtains that are all drawn. The room is very dark, lit only by a slit of light where the curtains don't quite meet. The room gives the impression of a cave. There is a large Jackson Pollack painting on the wall—"Number 15, 1949" to be exact. The living room has a bar. The floor is like an obstacle course, littered with dirty dishes, liquor bottles, glasses, and clothing. It is the scene of a ten-day binge. MARTY is in a heap just inside the door, where DEL has half-dragged her. DEL crosses to the curtains and pulls one to the side. MARTY, shielding her eyes, lets out a cry.

MARTY: Too bright! *God dammit! (DEL pulls it hastily shut again.)*

DEL: Where's the lights, then? *(MARTY hits a switch by the door where she is now slumped. The room is now moderately lit, and DEL surveys it.)* Quite a party.

MARTY: *(Eyes still closed.)* That's Jackson Pollack.

DEL: Where?

MARTY: *(Not pointing.)* There.

DEL: I don't see anybody.

MARTY: On the wall… *(DEL glances at the canvas of paint drippings, not impressed.)*

DEL: Oh, yeah. I got one of them.

MARTY: *(Opening one eye, surprised.)* Really?

DEL: Yeah. Mine is titled "Drop Cloth." Where's the dogs…? The corgis?

MARTY: Priscilla took them.

DEL: She left? *(MARTY crosses unsteadily to the couch, shoves some bottles out of the way, and collapses. DEL spots the bar.)* A bar? In the *living room*? You gotta be kiddin' me… That's handy.

MARTY: We like to entertain… *(Suddenly straightening.)* I never invited you in.

DEL: Do you want me to leave? *(Silence as MARTY picks up an LP and studies the cover. It's the 1955 album "Anita." DEL watches her for a moment.)* Yeah… I'm gonna make some coffee. *(She exits toward the kitchen. Tripping over the bottles, MARTY crosses slowly to the stereo, clutching the album. Gingerly, she puts the record on the turntable and turns on the stereo. The song "Honeysuckle Rose" begins to play. MARTY sways unsteadily for a few moments. DEL re-enters.)*

MARTY: Anita O'Day… *(Giving DEL a knowing look, as she sings along.)* She's one of us…

DEL: A drunk?

MARTY: *(MARTY stops and stares at DEL.)* That, too. *(Attempting to be seductive, she sings the lyrics in an unfocused, way. DEL watches her.)* You know, Anita wouldn't wear an evening gown. Band singer for Gene Krupa, and she wouldn't wear an evening gown. Made him give her a band jacket... so she could be one of the guys... *(She points this to DEL.)*

DEL: Okay. *(Crossing over and snapping off the stereo.)* Let's call your sponsor.

MARTY: Oh, let's not.

DEL: Here... here's the telephone. *(Holding it out to her.)* You want me to dial...?

MARTY: No... *(She takes the phone and puts it down.)* Do you know who my sponsor is?

DEL: No.

MARTY: Bill W... *Bill W.* "William...Griffith... *(Air quotes.)* ...W!*" Mr. AA, himself. *(She laughs.)* Still want me to call him...?

DEL: Yeah, I do. Where's his number? This your address book? *(She opens an address book and looks through it.)*

MARTY: *(Laughing.)* You want me to call the founder of Alcoholics Anonymous and tell him that his number-one recruiter is two weeks into a bender and three sheets to the wind...? *(She laughs raucously.)* You really want me to do that?

DEL: Yeah. *(MARTY crosses to the bar, shaking her head.)* Hey... hey... !

MARTY: *(Waving a hand dismissively.)* Hair of the dog. *(She pours herself something that's handy and downs it quickly.)*

DEL: Coffee's brewin.'

MARTY: Well, where the hell is it? *(DEL exits. MARTY crosses to a mirror to inspect the damage.)* Oh, Jesus… *(She backs away and then approaches again.)* God… Oh… *(She lights a cigarette and calls out to DEL.)* So what do you do…? *(She can't remember the name. She yells offstage.)* What's your name?

DEL: *(Offstage.)* "Del."

MARTY: *(Shouting.)* Del, what do you do?

DEL: *(Entering with a pot of coffee.)* I own a bar.

MARTY: *(Quoting DEL.)* That's handy.

DEL: I just sell the stuff. I don't drink it.

MARTY: Is it a bar for…*(Exaggerated enunciation.)* "…ho-mo-philes?"

DEL: It's a neighborhood bar. Anybody's welcome. But, yeah, I make it a safe place for the ladies. *(She hands MARTY a cup of coffee. MARTY looks at it and starts to gag. She runs offstage. Sound of vomiting. DEL sits. Silence. Sound of coughing. After a moment, she shouts.)* Hey…. Hey! You okay…? *(MARTY reels in and staggers toward the sofa.)*

MARTY: *(Swatting DEL angrily.)* Get off, get off, get off! *(DEL hops off the sofa and MARTY collapses on it, groaning. She is very, very sick. DEL looks at her and then crosses to the bar. She pours a glass with a small amount of whiskey and takes it to MARTY. MARTY drinks it. She collapses with some relief. DEL returns to her coffee, walking around the room. MARTY finally opens her eyes.)* Do you know who I am?

DEL: "Mrs. Mann." I came here to see you, remember?

MARTY: No— do you know *who* I am?

DEL: National Council on Alcoholism.

MARTY: But what I *do*?

DEL: *(Looking around.)* Well, you party…

MARTY: Two hundred and fifty speeches a year. A *year*. And there's only three hundred and sixty-five days in a year. *(Pause.)* Thirty-six thousand miles…   For *fifteen* years. *Fifteen!*

DEL: That's great. Now, let's call your sponsor…

MARTY: *(Rolling right on.)* Two hundred and fifty speeches times fifteen, times thirty-six thousand… How many people do you think that is? And that's not even counting the radio and the television …? How many people do you think are sober today because of Mrs. Marty Mann getting up in front of them and inspiring them with her sobriety. *(DEL picks up the telephone and holds out the receiver. MARTY takes it and starts talking without dialing.)* Hello…? Yes… *New York Times*…? Get me your news desk… *(She smiles at DEL. DEL rolls her eyes.)* Yes… All right… *(She smiles at DEL, who is not amused.)* Yes. I have a story for you. "Mrs. Marty Mann, founder of the National Council on Alcoholism, has fallen off the wagon…" and I've even got the headline for you: "The Shot Heard Round the World." *(MARTY starts laughing. DEL takes the phone and hangs it up.)* What? Isn't that what you want? The whole world to know?

DEL: No.

MARTY: Well, that's what's going to happen if I call Bill W., because he's going to make me go to a meeting. So what happens then? Word gets out and the NCA fires me. My own organization, and they fire me. And then where am I going to go? Fifty-six years old, and who's going to give me a job… you? *(DEL starts to say something, but she cuts her off.)* And *then…* then thousands—*hundreds* of thousands of men and women all over the world are going to say to themselves, "If Mrs. Mann, after twenty years in AA… if even *she* can't stay sober, what chance do I have?" And they'll give up. *(Snaps her fingers.)* Give up! *(Long silence.)* No, I am not going to call my sponsor. *(MARTY looks at DEL, challenging her.)*

DEL: Okay.

MARTY: *(Belligerent.)* What?

DEL: *(Deadpan.)* I don't know what to say …   You're so special. *(A long pause, possible showdown. Suddenly, MARTY starts laughing.)*

MARTY: Darn tootin' I am! 1939… *1939!* Went to my first meeting. There were only two of them then… one in Brooklyn… and one in Akron… O-hi-o. Nothing but men. Oh, goody! And they were not happy to see me, either… Told me I was too young, and too classy—and besides women couldn't be drunks.

DEL: Or soldiers.

MARTY: I had to prove it to them.

DEL: How about some coffee?

MARTY: You want to know what I did? I told them my story. *(DEL sighs and pours herself more.)* I was over in England, and it was a Fourth of July party—

DEL: *(Not looking up.)* They don't do Fourth of July.

MARTY: *(Confused.)* What?

DEL: *(Still not looking up.)* In England.

MARTY: Hm. *(A long silence.)* Well… it was the Fourth of July and it was a party. In England. *(She launches into her story. DEL listens impatiently.)* I was drinking, of course… two quarts of scotch on a good day. And apparently I had developed the blind staggers, because someone had walked me upstairs to my room… my room with a balcony overlooking the terrace where the party was. And I *may* have fallen, or I *may* have jumped… I don't remember which… but one way or the other, I made quite a splash on that stone terrace. Bit off both sides of my tongue, smashed all my lower teeth, and fractured *both* hinges of my jaw. Oh, and I also broke my leg and my hip. *(Pointing.)* Here… and here… and here… *(She pauses for effect. DEL looks at her watch.)* After I got out of surgery, I had the student nurses smuggle whiskey in for me. Had to drink it through a straw because they'd wired my jaw shut!

DEL: Yeah—

MARTY: *(Cutting her off.)* And *then,* after I got out of the hospital, I booked my passage back to the States on the *Queen Mary*. It was going to be my little floating rehab. My mother and my sister came to meet the boat in New York… freezing cold. It was December. Shivering together on that pier, they watched every single passenger get off that boat… and finally, after the whole kit-and-caboodle was empty and everybody was gone, they saw two stewards carrying something down the gangplank… a stretcher—with me on it! I was too drunk to even walk off the boat… *(Pause.)* So that's the story I told the men, and it shut 'em right up.

DEL: Bet it did. *(Rising.)* You want to know why I'm here? I'm here, because the cottage that's next to yours in Cherry Grove is for sale and I want to buy it.

MARTY: Barking up the wrong tree. It's not mine. Shelley Perkins owns it.

DEL: Yeah, I know, but she won't sell to me. She keeps tellin' me she's got a buyer, but the sign's been up for five months.

MARTY: She forgot to take it down. *(DEL looks at her. MARTY is distracted by the album cover.)*

DEL: The sign is still up, because there's no buyer. *(Pause.)* I said, *"There's no buyer."*

MARTY: *(Looking up.)* I don't know anything about it.

DEL: Oh, I think you do. *(Long pause.)*

MARTY: *(Pointing.)* Cigarette… *(DEL gets her one and lights it for her.)* Thank you. *(A pause. Flirtatiously.)* Del. *(She takes a drag and adopts a seductive pose.)* So when did you start coming to Cherry Grove?

DEL: Three years ago. 1957.

MARTY: *(Exhaling.)* Ah. The summer after Duffy's burned down… Duffy's was the hotel on the island. That was when everything changed… the last summer that Cherry Grove was really Cherry Grove. *(Watching the smoke from her cigarette.)* You know, that year the entire chorus of *My Fair Lady* came down… The whole summer was like one big Broadway musical… *(Singing seductively.)* *"We could have danced all night, we could have danced all night…"* *(DEL is not amused. MARTY rolls the tip of her cigarette in the ashtray.)* In the 30's and 40's, we used to get all the theatre people…

Hermione Gingold and Cheryl Crawford…and the writers… Carson McCullers, Patricia Highsmith, Jane Bowles, Tennessee Williams, Truman Capote… Who needed electricity when we had all that brilliance? The parties… My god… the parties… They all had these ridiculous themes… and the boys would spend weeks—*months!*—on their costumes… We would see them coming across on the ferry, hauling over these enormous feather boas, and hoop skirts, and fairy wings. And the biggest social event of the year was the Easter Sunday Hat Party at Duffy's. The boys would be wearing these magnificent *creations*… Us girls, of course… we would just slap on a golf visor and call it good. *(She laughs.)* It was like one big family… like a country club… and Duffy's was our clubhouse. *(She shakes her head.)* After the fire nothing was the same.

DEL: Today's Easter.

MARTY: Is it?

DEL: I took my girl to the service at St. John's.

MARTY: The girl I met?

DEL: Yeah, Flora's her name.

MARTY: Where is she?

DEL: She didn't want to stay. She didn't think I ought to bother you.

MARTY: Smart girl, that Flora.

DEL: Yeah, she is. Real smart. But she's wrong about this.

MARTY: About what?

DEL: Me comin' to see you.

MARTY: I told you I don't own that cottage.

DEL: Yeah, but you know the lady who does. You live next door to her. You're in the Cherry Grove Homeowners Association with her. *(MARTY looks at her. This is the showdown.)* Yeah, Flora's smart. She's had to be, because you see, she's my girl. And that little country club thing you just told me about…? Yeah, Flora already knew that was goin' on with your homeowners thing. 'Cause she's real smart about stuff like that. But, see, here's where she's wrong. She doesn't believe things ever change. But I see them changin' every day. And I think you do, too, with all those miles you got on you. People are changin' all over this country. And the Grove is changin,' too. And I know you know that… but Flora, she doesn't believe in it. I told her that you were gonna recommend us to your neighbor… That you were gonna tell Miss Perkins how she ought to sell to us, because we're a nice couple—sober, with good jobs… Flora's a teacher's aide and I own my own business. And I fix things. Was a carpenter in the Women's Army Corps. I'd keep the place up. Yeah, but see, Flora, she doesn't believe you'd do that for us. I told her she was wrong

MARTY: *(A long silence. MARTY looks up at the painting. This is an aggressive, intentionally patronizing demonstration of class privilege.)* A Jackson Pollack painting is not a drop cloth. Do you know why? Because every pigment on the canvas was put there intentionally. He chose his colors. He chose where he was going to fling them and how often and when to stop. He was looking for a dynamic but harmonious composition. That's all any of us can ask of life. He didn't invite his friends to come over and fling. He didn't put on a blindfold and pick his colors indiscriminately. There was intentionality in his community of design, however random it may appear to the untrained eye.

DEL: *(Getting hot under the collar.)* The Grove isn't a painting. It's a bunch of houses where lesbians don't have to hide.

MARTY: But where did that safety come from?

DEL: Numbers. Numbers like me and Flora.

MARTY: But originally… where did it come from *originally*? It was people who knew each other coming together to create a little village of like-minded souls. People with a vision and with initiative, and, of course, *capital*. And we created the Grove to reflect the world in which we wanted to live. A world that was bright and gay, colorful, light-hearted, and filled with tasteful art and music and theatre. Cherry Grove has an aesthetic that is like the Pollack painting… a spattering of many different colors, but all harmonious and representing the whole. But what would happen to that very carefully crafted design, those intentional patterns, if everybody got to, at random, fling themselves onto our canvas?

DEL: You gotta be kiddin' me.

MARTY: You have your community and we have ours.

DEL: No, see… "our…" "our" community. *Us.* Women who love women… *Our* community.

MARTY: Let me ask you something… Do you see anybody in "our" community at Cherry Grove who looks like you?

DEL: Not yet.

MARTY: Well, why do you think that is?

DEL: Not handsome enough?

MARTY: Try again. *(Pause. DEL waits. MARTY gets angry.)* No…? Well, maybe it's because we happen to have good jobs, good jobs that we worked our ass off to get. Jobs that pay us a lot of money, and jobs that, in return, expect our loyalty. They expect us to uphold their reputations, not get ourselves involved in any scandals or gossip, not do anything that would embarrass them. That's the price we pay for being *effective* in the world. That's why I can't call Bill. That's the price.

DEL: Yeah? And how's that workin' for you?

MARTY: That's none of your business, is it? But you're whining to me about why Shelly Perkins says she has a buyer when her sign is still up… It's because she wants to be sure that whoever buys that house is going to keep the neighborhood safe by protecting our anonymity, if you will. By not signaling to the whole world who we are and how we live our lives.

DEL: Oh, please.

MARTY: Not all of us own a bar where we can go to work dressed like a man—

DEL: *(Rising, angry.)* Hey, I dress like *me*! And you know something? You and your "blazer girls" with your lipstick and your high heels… You look ridiculous. You're not foolin' anybody. Signaling? You're all walkin' down the boardwalk holdin' up a giant sign that says, "I hate who I am."

MARTY: *(Smiling.)* But you think I should recommend you as a good neighbor…?

DEL: *(A beat.)* So you're not gonna do it…? Flora's right. You're not gonna help us, are you?

MARTY: *(Shrugging.)* Life on life's terms.

DEL: *(Infuriated.)* Yeah? Well, here's a little "life's terms" for *you….* you bitch! *(She holds up the address book.)* I got Bill W's number right here, and I'm gonna call him and tell him what his little sponsee's been up to!

MARTY: *(Grabbing the address book and throwing it.)* The hell you are! Get the hell out of my apartment!

DEL: *(Taunting.)* Columbus 3-5589.

MARTY: Get out or I'll call the police!

DEL: *(Picking up the phone and taking the phone off the receiver.)* Columbus 3-5589… *(She starts to dial.)*

MARTY: Oh, no you *don't!* *(MARTY rushes her.)*

DEL: *(Sidestepping the lunge.)* 3-5589…!

MARTY: Give me that fucking phone….! *(Screaming.)* Right now! You fucking bitch! *(DEL turns away from her, continuing to dial.)*

DEL: … 5589… *(MARTY, screeching, is trying to grab the phone. DEL keeps turning. They are both pushing and shoving each other. This is very close to an all-out physical fight. MARTY becomes entangled in the phone cord as DEL keeps turning and she keeps following.)* …5589… *(Suddenly MARTY starts to lose her balance. She screams and starts to fall.)*

MARTY: *(Terrified.) My hip! My hip! (Clutching at DEL.)* Oh, my god… my hip…!

DEL: Shit! *(DEL slams down the receiver and tries to grab MARTY.)* Shit...! *(They both fall. MARTY is screaming with rage and pain.)* Shit... Oh, fuck... Oh, fuck...

MARTY: Look what you did! I'm calling the police! Look what you did to me! *(Weeping in pain and frustration.)*

DEL: You want to get up?

MARTY: No... No... *Don't touch me!* I'm calling the police...

DEL: Ambulance? Do you want me to call an ambulance?

MARTY: Don't touch that phone! Don't you *dare* touch that fucking phone! I'm going to have you arrested! *(DEL doesn't say anything. MARTY rolls in pain.)* Hand me a pillow! *(DEL hands her a pillow.)* Both of them! *(DEL hands her all the pillows on the sofa. MARTY props up her back. She has begun to cry from pain and helplessness.)* Get me a drink... I need a drink! *(DEL stands helplessly.)* Get me a *fucking drink*, you bitch! You did this to me! *(Pause. She is really crying now, overwhelmed with self-pity, and also the fall is triggering a post-traumatic memory of the earlier fall.)* This is the hip I broke... They didn't set the bones right, and I had to have another operation when I got home... I couldn't straighten my legs... They made me wear these horrible weights... for years... *(She is pleading.)* It hurts... It hurts...!

DEL: I'm sorry. Let me call an ambulance...

MARTY: Fuck you! *(She rolls over and is crying and moaning like a child. DEL is quite frightened.)*

DEL: Look, Mrs. Mann... I don't know what to do.

MARTY: *Leave me alone! Go the hell away!*

DEL: I can't do that. Let me call someone. I don't know what to do. Is there someone I can call…?

MARTY: No! There's no one! There's *no one*! *(Sobbing.)*

DEL: I'll call my sponsor. I won't tell her your name, I promise. I can't leave you like this. *(MARTY is whimpering. Gingerly DEL crosses to the phone.)* I'm going to call my sponsor now. I'm not going to call anyone else. I swear. I don't know what to do… *(Pause. DEL dials her sponsor's number. During this call MARTY gets quieter and quieter.)* Hello… Frankie? *(MARTY lifts her head. DEL turns toward her and points at the phone.)* It's Frankie, my sponsor… *(Back to Frankie)* Frankie? Del, yeah. I'm in trouble… What? No, I'm not drinking… No… No… I'm at this lady's apartment and she's on a binge, and she fell and I can't tell if she's hurt—

MARTY: *(Screaming loudly enough to be heard on the other end of the line.)* I'm *hurt*! I'm fucking *hurt*, and you *did* it, you *bitch*…!

DEL: *(MARTY gets very quiet during this call.)* I can't tell how bad she's hurt, but she won't let me call an ambulance… *(Brief pause.)* What? No, I'm not her sponsor… *(Brief pause.)* No… I don't know her—*(Pause.)* Listen, Frankie—she's fallen on her hip, and it's the hip she broke before and—*(Brief pause.)* What? *(Pause. DEL is exasperated.)* What am I doin' here? I'm *here*, because I came by to talk to her about the cottage in Cherry Grove… the one I want to buy. I told you about that. But that's got nothing to do with this. She's on the floor and—*(Brief pause.)* WHAT? *(Pause.)* Goddam, it Frankie! I got a crisis goin' on here, and I'm callin' you for help! *(Pause.)* I *told* you… I came here to talk to her about the goddam cottage... Will you listen to me? *(Pause.)* Oh, for chrissake… I was tryin' to get her to recommend me and

Flora to the owner... okay? *(Brief pause.)* Flora? Where's Flora? How the fuck would I know? Home... She got pissed and went home. *(Brief pause. DEL is really upset.)* I don't know why she's pissed. She's Flora, okay? *(Pause.)* No... wait! Don't hang up. I'm listenin...' Frankie, I'm listenin.' *(Pause.)* Okay... Flora thought it was a dumb idea, me comin' over here. *(Pause.)* Yeah... because she's had some bad experiences... *(DEL suddenly stops, slowly lowering the receiver.)* Oh, shit. Oh, shit... *(Hand to her head.)* Oh, man... *(Lifting receiver again.)* Frankie, I am in trouble... Oh, man, I am in so much trouble... Flora was tryin' to tell me this thing that was really important— like the worst thing that ever happened to her... Frankie, it was *bad*... and I didn't even listen... and she was cryin'... and I was just all about the fuckin' cottage... Oh, man... Frankie, I'm such an asshole... Oh, man... Flora's never gonna forgive me.... Oh, shit... *(Long pause.)* Yeah... Yeah... *(DEL looks at her watch.)* Yeah. I can make it to that meeting. I'll get a crosstown bus... Oh, shit... Yeah... Thanks... Oh, man, Frankie... you're savin' my life... Yeah... See you there. *(She hangs up and turns to look at MARTY, who is lying quietly on the floor with her eyes closed. She takes a deep breath.)* I'm goin' to a meetin.' *(Silence.)* I can take you if you want to go. *(Pause.)* We can call a cab. *(MARTY rolls over and looks at her.)* I'm sorry I barged in on you. That wasn't right. I shouldn't have done that. *(Silence. DEL collects the phone and the address book and sets them next to MARTY.)* Here's the phone and your address book...

MARTY: *(Immobile, eyes still closed.)* It's the shame isn't it?

DEL: *(Turning, distracted.)* What?

MARTY: *(Opening her eyes.)* The shame.

DEL: *(Impatient.)* *What's* the shame?

MARTY: The bad thing that happened… to your girlfriend—

DEL: *(Stopped in her tracks. Long pause.)* Yeah. *(A realization.)* Yeah, I guess it is.

MARTY: *(Nodding.)* It's always the shame… *(DEL is still frozen.)* Help me onto the sofa before you go.

DEL: *(Breaking out of her reverie.)* Oh… sure. *(She crosses to MARTY and helps her to the sofa. She freezes again, lost in thought.)*

MARTY: Aren't you catching a bus?

DEL: *(Still puzzling it out.)* She didn't want my sympathy…

MARTY: *(Laughing.)* Of course she didn't! *(DEL looks at her.)* I lost a girlfriend to shame once.

DEL: You did?

MARTY: Oh, yes... But you have your bus to catch.

DEL: How did you lose her?

MARTY: *(Taking a minute to appraise DEL's sincerity.)* You really want to hear the story?

DEL: Yeah. I do. *(DEL sits.)*

MARTY: Well… we were young… *so* young… fourteen, both of us. She lived next door to me… in Chicago. And we were so in love. We really were. *So* in love… *(Shaking her head at the memory.)* And then we were diagnosed with tuberculosis. Both of us. And that was shameful… shameful for our families, because in 1918, tuberculosis was something associated with filth and squalor. Nice people didn't get tuberculosis. If someone in your family had TB, it was an appalling secret, and you just didn't let anyone know.... So Katherine's family shut her up in her bedroom on the second floor and told everyone she was away, visiting friends. And they didn't tell her what she had. Nobody told me either, but my family sent me to a place in California... It was new, experimental. They were taking TB patients and treating us with sunshine, and clean air, and fresh food. I remember they would bring me this drink every afternoon, milk with raw eggs mixed in. And every afternoon, I would get out of bed, and walk the glass over to the window, and dump it out. One day the doctor called me in to his office, and he told me that I had tuberculosis and that it was a very serious disease that could kill me, and that it was important for me to drink the egg mixture every day if I wanted to get better. So... finally... after all those months of silence and secrecy and feeling confused and angry and ashamed... well, it was like someone just turned on a light and suddenly everything made sense. It was so simple and so clear. And of course, I drank the damned eggs and I started doing everything they told me, and I got well. Katherine, of course, didn't.

DEL: I'm sorry.

MARTY: *(Proud of her amends.)* Well, you may be sober today because she died. *(Pause.)* You see, it was the shame, not the tuberculosis, that killed her... the ignorance and the shame. And, I realized it was the same with alcoholism, and that what we needed was a national agency educating people that it was a disease, not a moral condition... that alcoholics didn't need to be ashamed.

DEL: *(A long pause. DEL nods.)* Thank you. *(DEL rises and crosses to the door.)*

MARTY: *(Musing.)* It's always the shame...

DEL: *(From the doorway.)* Take care, Mrs. Mann. *(She exits. After DEL leaves, MARTY looks around and rises from the sofa. Her hip really does hurt. She crosses slowly to the window and pulls one of the curtains to the side, letting in a brilliant shaft of light that strikes the telephone where it is on the floor. MARTY registers the theatricality of this with a snort. She crosses to the telephone and looks at it for a moment. Slowly, she picks it up. She dials a number.)*

MARTY: *(This is a strenuous performance.)* Hello…? Rebecca… I'm so glad I got you… I'm so sick… I'm *really* sick… *(Becoming weepy.)* I need help. *(Pause.)* It's the flu… I've been in bed for a week, and Priscilla's away. It's been awful… I haven't been able to do anything. *(She begins to cry.)* Rebecca, I need help… Can you come get me? *(Speaking rapidly.)* I just need to go out to the country, to your farm for a couple of weeks… just get away from everything… just get out to the country… get away… get away from people, away from work… clean air and fresh food… sunshine… *(Pause.)* No, I'm too sick to take the train… *(Pause.)* Please, Rebecca… I'm so sick… the flu… *(Pause.)* Oh, thank god! And, please, don't tell anyone. I don't want anyone bothering me… Don't tell anyone… *(Pause.)* Yes… yes… I'll go pack right now… Remember, don't tell anyone…. *(She hangs up the phone with a groan of relief: That took a lot of energy. Crossing to the bar, she pours herself another shot of whiskey, drinks it, and slowly begins to collect the bottles on the floor.)*

Blackout

End of Play

Lighting Martha

A One-Act Play

Cast of Characters

JEAN ROSENTHAL: The legendary lighting designer, 55. Deeply private.

MIKI KINSELLA: Her partner and assistant, 45. Aggressively devoted to Jean.

BEN: Lighting technician, 60's.

Scene

The stage of New York City Center.

Time

April 30, 1969, late night after the final dress rehearsal for Martha Graham's premiere of *The Archaic Hours*.

Lighting Martha

The darkened stage of New York City Center. It is late at night, April 30, 1969, after the final dress rehearsal for Martha Graham's production, The Archaic Hours. *Everyone has gone home and the theatre is dark. The stage is lit with work lights. There is a single, unlit ghost light to the side. MIKI KINSELLA, 45, stands completely still at center stage, clutching a clipboard and gazing out over the empty theatre. Her life partner is days from dying, and their lesbian relationship cannot be publicly recognized. The partner has forbidden MIKI to talk about her disease or her dying, and MIKI is at a breaking point with repressed grief and rage. BEN, 60, enters. He's a lighting technician. Believing he is alone in the theatre, BEN is humming tunelessly to himself as he crosses upstage of MIKI. He is startled to see her.*

BEN: Miki…? *(Louder.)* Miki? *(She turns.)* I thought you had left… *(MIKI turns wordlessly to look at BEN. He is disconcerted by her silence.)* I thought you left with Jean… *(More silence.)* Are you okay?

MIKI: *(Responding with aggression.)* Sure… Sure, why wouldn't I be?

BEN: *(Smiling.)* The lighting looks great.

MIKI: *(Caustic.)* Of course it does… "Lighting by Jean Rosenthal." The "best on Broadway"… The best in the world! The woman who single-handedly invented the whole field of lighting design. Of course it looks great.

BEN: *(Confused by her aggression.)* Want me to call you a cab…? *(Long silence. He changes tack.)* That was a pretty special dress rehearsal tonight. I don't think anybody on the crew expected to see Jean here.

MIKI: *(Her anger building.)* Why not? She told Martha she would light the show. Why wouldn't you expect her for the final dress rehearsal? She's lit every Graham season for the past thirty-four years. Hasn't missed a one.

BEN: Well, Jean is… you know… *(MIKI's not helping him.)* She's pretty sick, isn't she?

MIKI: "*Sick?*" *(Exploding.)* She's dying, Ben. *Dying*. And *soon*. My partner is dying. *(Turning toward the house, she yells.) Jean Rosenthal is dying! (Turning back to BEN, she smiles.)* I'm not allowed to say that. *Nobody* is allowed to say it, especially her goddam doctors. She makes them all talk to me. She says "Oh, talk to Miki about everything, and then *she* can tell me." And then she says to me, "I don't want to know. I don't want to know *anything*." It's been like that for the entire last year.

BEN: *(Musing.)* Dying…

MIKI: Dying.

BEN: Well, the crew figured it must be pretty bad, her showing up at City Center tonight in an ambulance…

MIKI: *(Cutting him off.)* Oh, dear God…! The ambulance… and then wheeling her in on a gurney. On a *gurney*! The woman is too damn sick to use a wheelchair, you'd think they'd realize she's too sick to come to work! You'd think they'd have more sense than to let her come at all! You'd think they'd keep her in the goddam hospital! But then *somebody* had the bright idea to bring her on a *gurney*! I don't' know what genius came up with that—

BEN: *(Thoughtfully.)* Could have been Jean…

MIKI: *(Ignoring him.)* And those goddam doctors! Letting her do it! Signing her out! I told them not to, but do they listen to me? Who am I? Just her "lighting assistant?" Her "friend?" Her "roommate?" Why should they listen to me? They all do what Jean says. She always gets her way.

BEN: *(Nodding.)* Oh, yeah. Jeannie gets her way.

MIKI: *(On a tear now.)* Weeks to live…*weeks*! Maybe *days*! And *Martha*! *(She begins to pace.)* I just… I can't even… Martha could have stopped it! She is the only person who could. She's the boss. Martha could have told Jean that she would not allow her in the door at City Center. But did she stop it? No! She *encouraged* her! Standing there, next to that goddam gurney… and Jean—Jean, what—? Weighing seventy pounds and barely able to hold herself up, and Martha's got her bending backwards to check the positions of the lights! I never saw anything so selfish in my life! Like there couldn't be anything more important going on in the universe than lighting Martha Graham. That woman is the most selfish, the most egotistical—

BEN: *(Uncomfortable, he interrupts MIKI's outburst.)* Hey— hey, Miki! Let me call you a cab.

MIKI: No, no… *(Still pacing furiously.)*

BEN: C'mon Miki… It's been a long night.

MIKI: *(Turning on him.)* Where would I go, Ben? Where would I go? Back to the apartment? Her stuff all over the place, and she's never coming home. *She's never coming home!* What am I supposed to do with all that *stuff*… ? *(Her voice has begun to get shaky, but she rallies with anger.)* I don't know what she wants me to do with it, because, God knows, we can't talk about it! Her doctors can't talk about it! Nobody can talk—

BEN: *(Cutting her off.)* Hey! I've got an idea… How about we go somewhere and I buy you a beer?

MIKI: *(She stops pacing and looks at him, suddenly drained.)* No, you go on. You have a show tomorrow.

BEN: So do you.

MIKI. Yeah…

BEN: You know Jeannie's gonna be okay…

MIKI: Ben, she's *dying.*

BEN: Yeah, she is, and she knows it. But she's tough. *(Passing her a flask.)*

MIKI: *(Ignoring the flask.)* I don't know that she's as tough as you think.

BEN: *(Taking a drink himself and then holding it out again.)* How long have you known her?

MIKI: Since 1956. Thirteen years. *(A beat.)* My lucky number. *(She looks at the flask, reconsiders, and takes a swig.)* I worked with her on *West Side Story.*

BEN: *(Nodding)* Yeah?

MIKI: *(Remembering as she takes another drink.)* Cabaret, Hello, Dolly!, Barefoot in the Park… and of course Martha's company… every goddam year… every single goddam—

BEN: Oh, yeah? *(Repossessing the flask.)* I've known Jeannie over thirty years... since the Depression... I met her over at Federal Theatre 891... with Orson Welles. Jeannie was just a kid, but, boy, she stepped right up. Houseman had made her his assistant. And then, when we all lost our jobs for doing that crazy show... the one that got banned... *(Searching his memory.)*

MIKI: *Cradle...*

BEN: Yeah, yeah. *The Cradle Will Rock...* Well, after that, we all went over to the Mercury Theatre with Orson. *(A snort.)* Orson. Ever work with him...?

MIKI: Before my time.

BEN: Oh, yeah. Right. Well, Orson, he always tried to take credit for everything. *(Shaking his head.)* It was Jean who lit *Caesar.* It was Jean who figured out how to do the scene changes without a curtain... the pools of light, the angles ... all Jean. But Orson wouldn't give her the credit ... He called her his "lighting manager, " but I'm telling you, she designed it. She designed the hell out of it. We were all just electricians before Jeannie came along. She was the artist...

MIKI: "Was..."

BEN: *(Still remembering.)* And the guys in the union gave her hell, pure hell... They didn't want to work with a woman and they sure as shootin' weren't going to take orders from one either. They just gave her hell... But she was tough... They'd use the worst language, tell the dirtiest jokes, trying to break her... and they could be kind of rough, too... Shoving her out of the way, knocking her down, acting like they didn't see her. Up in the rigging, too. I remember the day one of the guys didn't like her telling him how to do his job. He said if she did it again, he'd throw his hammer at her. And he did, too. But she stuck it out.

MIKI: I would've had their asses fired so fast... *(She takes the flask back and takes another swig.)*

BEN: You couldn't... not thirty years ago. Jeannie just had to ride it out. But she never let them see she was mad. She never raised her voice. And the more they disrespected her, the more she went out of her way to treat them with courtesy. You know she was always real careful not to embarrass us. If there was somebody doing something the wrong way... she'd just take the guy over to the side, like she was having some kind of professional consult with him... and that's when she'd tell him. Making sure nobody else could hear what she was saying. That made an impression. You bet it did. Oh, yeah.

MIKI: Saint Rosenthal. *(A toast.)* Our Lady of the Lights.

BEN: You know how, when she comes through the door, you hear someone yell out, "Jean's in the house...?"

MIKI: Yeah...

BEN: Well, that's so the boys all know to clean up their language. Some new guy starts mouthing off in front of her, we straighten him out real fast.

MIKI: But, Ben, you let her come here tonight on a gurney. On a fucking *hospital gurney*!

BEN: Miki, she wanted it that way... *(MIKI, turns away, fighting back tears. Long pause.)* C'mon... let me get you a cab...

MIKI: No. I'm okay. *(Handing back the flask without turning.)* You go on home.

BEN: It's not good to be by yourself.

MIKI: There's worse things than being alone, trust me…. Don't worry about me. Hey, I even got me a ghost light. *(She crosses over to the ghost light, still hiding her face from him. She switches it on.)* I bet the dead are a hell of a lot more fun than the dying.

BEN: You sure? *(No response.)* Okay. *(He starts to leave, halts, and then sets the flask on the floor as he exits. On the way out BEN throws the breakers. There is a loud clang as the stage goes dark except for the illumination from the ghost light.)*

MIKI: *(Turning to see if he's gone, MIKI notices the flask, and retrieves it. She addresses the empty theatre.)* Well, come on, all you theatre ghosts… Don't mind me… Just pretend I'm not here. That's what I intend to do. *(Stretching out on the stage, she falls asleep. JEAN ROSENTHAL enters. This is Jean from 1967, before the cancer. She's in her mid-fifties and in good health. She walks up to the ghost light, holding her hands, palms outward, as if she was warming them in a fire. JEAN, who experiences light as tactile, caresses the edges of the light. She looks toward the sleeping MIKI, smiles and crosses down to her. Sitting cross-legged on the floor, she looks at MIKI. Slowly MIKI opens her eyes. She is momentarily confused.)* Jean…? *(JEAN waves a hand.)* This is a dream. *(JEAN smiles.)* Yeah, this is definitely a dream… You're not dying. You're not skinny enough. The real Jean is back at the hospital. *(She rolls over, turning her back on JEAN.)*

JEAN: "The real Jean…?"

MIKI: Yeah. *(Pause.)* The nightmare Jean. The Jean that isn't even Jean anymore. But she is.

JEAN: I know. I see her, too.

MIKI: *(MIKI rolls back to look at JEAN. She studies her for a moment.)* What are you? *(JEAN smiles and points toward the ghost light.)* Ah. The ghost light... *(Sitting upright.)* Wait! Is Jean... is she... ?

JEAN: No... No, she's still alive.

MIKI: But you're her ghost...?

JEAN: Well... More the form of her spirit.

MIKI: Doesn't that mean...?

JEAN: Sometimes, if there is something that needs to be taken care of... something urgent—the spirit can appear before the actual death.

MIKI: What is it? *(Uncomfortable, JEAN crosses away from MIKI to the front of the stage, looking at the lighting.)* Tell me why you're here!

JEAN: *(Referring to the lights.)* We did a nice job, didn't we?

MIKI: We? *I* did most of the work. You were too sick. Tell me what this thing is... this thing that's so urgent a ghost has come calling.

JEAN: Spirit. *(A beat.)* Miki... I'm going to need a little time.

MIKI: You don't have any. You'd know that if you talked to your doctors.

JEAN: *(Looking at the lights again.)* They look really good.

MIKI: *(Angry.)* I wish to hell I hadn't agreed to do it!

JEAN: Why?

MIKI: *(Rising and really beginning to engage.)* Because you wouldn't have taken the job without me, and it was too much! *(Shaking her head.)* It was too goddam much…

JEAN: But I promised Martha. I couldn't let her down.

MIKI: You couldn't let her down? Why not? Why the hell not? You don't owe that woman a thing! She owes *you*! Thirty-five years of lighting her shows. She should have come to the hospital tonight, instead of you and that damn ambulance coming to City Center… *(Pacing.)* Thirty-five years is not enough, but that vampire has to drain your last ounce of lifeblood, your last… your last… *(MIKI is so angry she can't find words.)* …everything! *(She stops and confronts JEAN.)* You don't owe Martha Graham a goddam thing!

JEAN: *(Quietly)* Miki… I do.

MIKI: No! I don't want to hear it. Not after tonight… Not after this… this… ghoulish pageant… ambulance, gurney, a Greek chorus of orderlies and nurses… everything but the professional mourners… Oh, I guess that was *me*, because it certainly wasn't Martha! *She's* got a show to do! God forbid your decaying body should get in the way of *her* dress rehearsal. *(JEAN looks away.) What*? What the hell could you possibly owe that woman?

JEAN: Being "Jean Rosenthal."

MIKI: More like she owes you for making her "Martha Graham."

JEAN: Miki, she—

MIKI: *(Holding up her hand.)* No! I don't want to hear it!

JEAN: All right… *(Long pause.)* …But—

MIKI: No! *(A beat.)* No… *(Long pause.)*

JEAN: Just one thing—

MIKI: I said I don't want to hear it! Not after tonight… *(Long, long silence. JEAN turns to leave. MIKI capitulates.)* Okay. But just one thing.

JEAN: I danced with her.

MIKI: You did not.

JEAN: She said I had peasant feet.

MIKI: No.

JEAN: It was a compliment.

MIKI: I don't believe you. *(JEAN looks at her.)* When?

JEAN: Before you were born.

MIKI: *(Annoyed.)* When?

JEAN: 1929.

MIKI: *(Defensively.)* I was five years old. *(JEAN smiles. Long silence.)* All right. Why were you dancing with Martha Graham?

JEAN: Because I couldn't get into college. None of them would have me, because of all the experimental schools I had gone to. So my parents sent me to the Neighborhood

Playhouse School. They thought it might broaden my horizons. *(JEAN smiles.)*

MIKI: And you signed up for Martha's dance class…

JEAN: I didn't have a choice! They made me! They made everybody take everything! That's how the Playhouse was… The set designers had to study dance, and the dancers had to study voice, and they made all the actors learn musical composition. It was crazy… You should have seen us—

MIKI: *(Suddenly overwhelmed, she reaches for her.)* Jean… I miss you—

JEAN: *(Quickly moving away.)* Don't!

MIKI: Why?

JEAN: It's a spirit thing… You can't touch me.

MIKI: Oh. "A ghost thing…" *(MIKI crosses away. JEAN watches her with compassion. MIKI turns, angry.)* What are you doing here? What the hell are you doing here?

JEAN: *(Long silence.)* Really, Miki… you should have seen us… There we were, all us teenaged girls… with our chic, little, bobbed haircuts and our shapeless, little sack-dresses… thinking we were the cat's pajamas… so worldly and so sophisticated… and then…

MIKI: Yeah. "Then Martha."

JEAN: *(Turning to look at her. MIKI does not take her eyes off JEAN during this speech.)* She threw open that classroom door and just stood there… that long black hair halfway down her back, and this… this robe…! Yards and yards of fabric… She had made it herself. It didn't look like anything that anyone was wearing in 1929. She was like some kind of priestess from another dimension. You know what it was? She was *feral*. That's what it was. She had not been domesticated. She was standing outside of everything that we thought mattered. And suddenly it was as if all of us girls were just little paper dolls lying flat in a box, waiting for someone to pick us up and play with us. Imagine meeting Martha Graham when you were young!

MIKI: *(Attempting to redirect the conversation.)* I met *you* when I was young.

JEAN: *(Lost in the memory.)* She told us that we were not here to please the audience. *(She turns to MIKI.)* Imagine a young girl hearing those words forty years ago… "We are not here to please the audience." She said that ugliness, if it had a powerful voice, was beautiful. Strength was the thing. She was so incredibly strong.

MIKI: *You're* the strongest woman I ever met.

JEAN: I remember that first day so clearly. She told us to take off our shoes and lie down on our backs. All twenty of us girls… lying on the floor. And then suddenly, she shouted "Contract!" And we all contracted. And then she shouted "Release!"… and we all released. "Contract!" "Release!" "Contract!" "Release!" Over and over… And while we're doing this, Martha delivers a sermon about how all movement begins in the "house of pelvic truth."

MIKI: *(Shaking her head.)* "The house of pelvic truth…"

JEAN: *(Playfully intimate.)* Well, I thought I had died and gone to heaven.

MIKI: No doubt.

JEAN: There's no going back from that house of pelvic truth.

MIKI: *(Ruefully.)* Don't I know it. *(MIKI reaches for JEAN's hand, but JEAN pulls it away. MIKI watches her.)* So you had a crush on Teacher.

JEAN: Huge. I fell down a flight of stairs for her.

MIKI: Pretty serious.

JEAN: I accidentally-on-purpose injured my back so I couldn't dance anymore and Martha would have to take me on as her technical assistant.

MIKI: Clever.

JEAN: It was my job to get her whatever she needed. And one day the "thing" that Martha needed was light. *(JEAN is overwhelmed with wonder by the memory.)*

MIKI: *(Turning away suddenly.)* I don't want to talk about her anymore. *(JEAN lowers her head and looks at her hands.)* What about *us… You*? Jean, you're *dying*, but you won't let us talk about it, and now it's too late. You're drugged and sleeping all the time. There's nothing but pain. There's nothing left to say. *(JEAN doesn't say anything.) You're leaving me!* Do you even love me?

JEAN: *(Protesting.)* Of course.

MIKI: What do you mean, "of course?"

JEAN: *(Pleading.)* We live together. You're my assistant… We've been working together for—

MIKI: *Exactly*! Your *assistant*! I'm your *assistant*! And how handy to live with your *assistant*! Just like Nan Porcher before me… Why, it's like having your own personal employee seven days a week, twenty-four hours a day…!

JEAN: Miki—

MIKI: No, I'm serious.

JEAN: We're lovers!

MIKI: Maybe that's just part of the job description.

JEAN: Don't be cruel, Miki.

MIKI: Me? Me "don't be cruel?" How about you making all the doctors talk to me? *I'm* the one who has to hear about the tumors and the blood tests, and where it's metastasized to, and how sick the radiation is going to make you, and how long you have to live. You don't want to hear any of it, so you make me hear it.

JEAN: Stop, Miki!

MIKI: You want to know how long you have to live?

JEAN: No! Stop it! *(Covering her ears.)*

MIKI: *(Pursuing her.)* You want to know?

JEAN: Stop! Stop!

MIKI: Two weeks. *(Raising her voice.) Two weeks! (JEAN has retreated. For MIKI, a dam has broken.)* I'm *not* sorry! I'm sorry I didn't say it sooner! Jean, we've been living a goddam lie… Pretending I'm your roommate, pretending I'm just your assistant… pretending you don't have cancer, pretending you're not dying! *(She looks at JEAN defensively.)* I don't care! You know what it's like? It's like the time you

116

were hired to light the tour of those Russian ballet dancers… Nijinsky's sister… remember? You told me her choreography was all in the first ten feet of the stage, because all they had in their theatres were gas footlights. *(Indicating their locations.)* So that's what they asked for… just to light those first ten feet… *(Indicating the positions of these lights.)* First pipe and two booms…That's what they wanted. But you… *you* needed to light behind them and around them and above them, because that's what Martha had taught you… that every area of the stage was important… that wherever she was dancing, *that* was center stage. But what would be the point of that with these Russian dancers, because they *couldn't* dance where you wanted to light them? And in the end, they threw you out. And now you've lit just this narrow, little strip of your life—what's left of it—and you've made both of us dance in that strip. Jean, you are dying! You are leaving! There is so much space—*so much space*—behind us and around us and above us, and *we can't move in it*! This flat little dance of denial right out in front of everybody… that's all you want to light! I can't do it anymore! I have things to say and do that are all over the place! All over the place, Jean! I can't do the goddam footlights dance anymore, and you won't move the booms for me!

JEAN: *(Anguished.)* I *can't* move the booms.

MIKI: You always say, "Your lighting will expose you." Well, it has. You don't love me. *You don't love me*. You never loved me. All you love is the work… the work and *Martha*!

JEAN: Miki, please…

MIKI: What? Do you want to run over the light cues again? After all, what could be more important than lighting Martha? *(She grabs her clipboard.)* Which cues did you want to look at, Miss Rosenthal?

JEAN: No, Miki…

MIKI: Not the cues? How about the lighting positions then? Where should we start…?

JEAN: Please…

MIKI: Oh, let's start here… The first pipe… Those precious first ten feet… that's what really counts. That's what's important—

JEAN: *(In agony.)* No! Stop it…! *(The ghost light suddenly cuts out, plunging the stage into near-total darkness. JEAN retreats to the shadows. A long silence.)*

MIKI: Jean…? Jean…? *(Long silence.)* Shit. *(She shouts into the theatre.)* I'm sorry! I'm sorry, I'm sorry, I'm sorry…! It's been a long night… an *endless* night! It's been the worst night of my fucking life…! And I know you came here to tell me something—or to do something—important… and I just… I'm sorry… Please come back.

JEAN: *(Stepping out from the shadows.)* I never left.

MIKI: *(Quickly.)* I'll get the light… *(MIKI starts to cross to the ghost light.)*

JEAN: *No, don't! (MIKI turns.)* Leave it off… please.

MIKI: But I thought ghosts—

JEAN: I like the dark. It reminds me of the light booth.

MIKI: Ah. *(A beat.)* The light booth… Oh, my god, Jean… How many hours, days… how many *years* of our lives have we spent together in a lightbooth?

JEAN: Why don't we imagine that we're in one now? *(She crosses next to MIKI.)*

MIKI: *(She looks at JEAN. Long silence. Nodding, MIKI turns to face the empty theatre.)* Okay. We're in a lightbooth together. So… what's the play?

JEAN: Well, it's about two women. They've been together for a long time. One of them is very sick and in this scene, she is lying on a bed.

MIKI: Or a gurney…

JEAN: The other woman is her partner—

MIKI: Her assistant.

JEAN: *(Reproving her gently.)* Miki…

MIKI: Okay… Two women… *Partners…*

JEAN: And they really need to talk, but they can't really see each other.

MIKI: Why not?

JEAN: Because the scene hasn't been properly lit.

MIKI: And whose fault is that? *(A beat.)* Sorry. *(Pause. MIKI adopts a professional attitude.)* Okay. So… two women, one in the bed, the other not… Why can't we just bring up the front light on the bed?

JEAN: Well… that's going to be a problem, because the woman—the one who is sick—doesn't want to be seen.

MIKI: Why not?

JEAN: Well… If she answers that question, she's going to be seen.

MIKI: *(A long pause. MIKI is starting to understand.)* Yeah. That's a problem. That's a *real* problem. *(JEAN nods.)* But what about backlighting? If we backlit her, that wouldn't put a light directly on her, but we could still make out her profile.

JEAN: *(Considering.)* That could work…

MIKI: Okay… backlighting, then? *(JEAN nods.)* The woman who is sick… her family were immigrants, weren't they?

JEAN: *(She takes a deep breath.)* Yes. Both her father and her mother came over from Romania with their families. They were both children… poor, not speaking English. And they had to work very hard. They worked all the time. It's who they were…

MIKI: *(Gazing at the imaginary scene.)* Okay. This is helping…

JEAN: *(Nodding, she resumes.)* Well… the father became an ear, nose and throat doctor, and the mother became a psychiatrist. And then they had children… two boys and a girl. And the parents and the boys… Well, they were all just incredibly strong-willed… And so the little girl learned that it was easier just to get out of their way… to stay in the shadows, to make herself invisible…

MIKI: *I* see you, Jean.

JEAN: *(A beat.)* And one of the schools they sent her to was out in the country… on a farm. It was kind of a socialist experiment. Everyone had to sleep in tents… and every morning somebody had to go to the henhouse and get the eggs for breakfast. And that could be pretty scary, so the girl learned how to get those eggs without disturbing the chickens… And that's how she survived the stage workers' union.

MIKI: People aren't chickens.

JEAN: But it was the same. The stagehands sat on their precious union jobs, just like hens guarding their eggs. They didn't want women coming in and "stealing" them… Miki, this is who I am. Working behind the scene, in the shadows. And when I got sick, I didn't want the doctors all studying me like I was a specimen—putting a spotlight on my body. It was unbearable! That's why I asked them to talk to you! I didn't mean to hurt you… I thought you would understand…

MIKI: *(Stricken.)* But I didn't… Oh, my god, I didn't get that at at all… Shit—

JEAN: Well, how could you? The woman in the bed doesn't want to be seen.

MIKI: *(Becoming agitated.)* No! No, look again! That's *not* the problem…! It's *not* the woman in bed. It's the other one! It's the *other one* who is the problem! *(She grabs the ghost light and turns it on, holding it very close to her face. The effect is alarming.)* It's the assistant—!

JEAN: Miki…

MIKI: No, look at her! She's the one who has been hiding! Hiding in plain sight. That's her strategy! Everyone thinking she's so devoted, so selfless… such a *martyr* to her famous partner! But *look at her*! She's an assistant because she doesn't want the responsibility! She doesn't want the responsibility for designing the lights… or designing her life!

She's a coward! A passive-aggressive, little coward who blames her brilliant, wonderful partner for everything in her life that isn't working!

JEAN: Oh, no, Miki, that's too harsh! Turn it off!

MIKI: A selfish coward!

JEAN: Oh, for heaven's sake—It isn't a melodrama! *(She reaches over and turns off the light.)* There are no villains or victims here. It's just an improperly lit scene. A glare is no better than the shadows, because it's *not about visibility* and it's not about melodrama, either. That was another century, but today, the whole purpose of stage lighting is to *aid communication*. That's what we're doing here… That's why I'm here. *(MIKI starts to protest.)* Listen to me, Miki… When I started working for Martha as her assistant, nobody— *nobody*—took her seriously. Nobody could see what she was doing in dance. They made fun of her… She wasn't pretty. She was too old. Her movements weren't graceful. That's what they saw. And Martha was in so much pain, because she was giving so much, and nobody could see it! And I was just aching to let her know that *I* saw her, and that *I* saw what she was doing and how important it was. Miki, I loved her so much I thought I would explode. And then she asked me to light her, and even though I was back in the shadows, I was able to take that love and just pour it all over her! I covered her with light; I caressed her with light… I tickled her and I teased her with light! I studied Martha so intimately, I could anticipate her movements, so that the light would be there just a split second before she needed it. And, Miki, she *received* it. She danced *with* my light, not just *in* it. I remember she told me she wanted this long, diagonal light that would start from the back of the stage and cross down to the front… And I designed it for her. She named it "the Finger of God," and Martha flirted with my Finger of God. At first, she would avoid it. She would work around it. And then she built it into the dance, into her character. My lighting became part of her struggle and search… and always, always, after approaching it and avoiding it… edging toward it, edging away… always, by the end of the dance, she would land right in the heart of it. You call this my work, but it's love. Miki, this *is* love to me, and when I asked you to be my assistant I thought I was sharing with you the greatest gift in the world.

MIKI: *(Stricken with guilt.)* I didn't deserve it.

JEAN: Miki—

MIKI: It's late… I should go. I have another ghost, tonight… in the hospital…

JEAN: Wait… *(A small light comes up on MIKI. MIKI turns to face it.)*

MIKI: What? *(Another light comes up on her, and then another. MIKI freezes.)*

JEAN: Can you feel it? *(More lights, shifting and changing.)* Can you feel the light?

MIKI: *(With a laugh.)* Jean, you are literally the only person on this whole planet who can feel light. *(A beat, as more lights shift and appear.)* Come here… Please. *(A pause.)* I'm not Martha. I don't want to be alone in the light. I need to share it with you. *(Slowly, JEAN steps out from the shadows and into the light with MIKI. More colors, more intensity, more movement. JEAN, facing the light, holds out her hands and closes her eyes, touching the light ecstatically. MIKI watches her from behind, overwhelmed.)*

JEAN: You really can't you feel this?

MIKI: *(Eyes only for JEAN.)* Yes. I believe I can. *(JEAN turns to look at her.)* I really can. Jeannie, it's beautiful. *(JEAN smiles and turns back to face the light. MIKI is suddenly overwhelmed with emotion.)* Oh, my god, I love you so much! *(She reaches her arms around JEAN to clasp her from behind. The stage is plunged into darkness.)* Jean…? Jean? *(MIKI crosses in the dark to the ghost light and switches it on. She glances around the stage, understanding that JEAN is gone. Turning to face the empty theatre, she looks up toward the lights, nodding with the relief of acceptance.)* "Lighting by Jean Rosenthal." *(She exits.)*

Blackout

End of Play

Female Nude Seated

A One-Act Play

<h1 style="text-align:center">Cast of Characters</h1>

MAINIE: A young Irish woman, 21, upper middle-class.

EVIE: A young Irish woman, 23, British landed gentry (upper class), disabled by polio.

<h2 style="text-align:center">Scene</h2>

Interior of a student's room in a rooming house in London near the Westminster School of Art.

<h2 style="text-align:center">Time</h2>

A late September night, 1917.

Seated Nude by Mainie Jellett
8.66 in. (22.00 cm.) (height) by 11.81 in. (30.00 cm.) (width)

Female Nude Seated

Lights come up on the interior of a room in a student rooming house near the Westminster School of Art in London. It's a late September night, 1917. The room is dimly lit from the glow of a streetlight outside the window. There is a figure asleep in a small bed. The room is furnished with a folding screen, a washstand with basin, and a wingback chair. The space is dominated by a tall, spectral form in the center of the room.

The woman in the bed begins to thrash. Suddenly she screams and sits up, panting. Overwhelmed with panic, she throws back the blankets and hurls herself out of the bed, tripping over clothing and other objects on the floor as she makes her way to a lamp and turns it on.

MAINIE is a young, upper-middle-class, Irish woman, 21, with bobbed hair. She wears an expensive nightgown. The ominous form is revealed to be a painter's easel that has been draped with a bed sheet. Next to the easel is a table covered with paints, with a handful of dirty brushes soaking in a jar. There is a bottle of turpentine on the table and a half-finished letter. The floor is littered with crumpled papers. MAINIE confronts the easel. Hysterical, she hesitates briefly before tearing the sheet off. The painting on the easel is a watercolor study of a young woman, nude, seated on a chair draped with blue cloth. [See "Seated Nude" by Mainie Jellett.]

Seeing the painting, MAINIE breaks down, half laughing and half crying. Still panting, she crosses to the window and throws it open. She leans far out of the window, taking great gulps of air. Calming down somewhat, she pulls back and turns to face the room.

Noticing the crumpled papers on the floor, she kicks one of them. MAINIE crosses to the table and looks at the half-written letter. She crumples it up and throws it on the floor with the others. With her face in her hands she doubles over, as if in physical pain. After a moment, she sits up with a sense of resolve. She picks up the jar with the brushes, and pulls them out. The solvent is muddy with mixed pigment. She lifts it as if to drink, reconsiders, and then rises to retrieve a fancy china cup and saucer. She pours the solvent into it. Bracing herself, she starts to lift the cup. There is a loud banging at the door. Screaming, she drops the cup, shattering it and spilling the contents onto herself and the floor.

EVIE: *(Offstage.)* Hello…?   Hello…? Open up!   Hello… ! *(More banging.)*   Hello…! *(MAINIE crosses to the door and unlocks it. EVIE HONE, 23, stands in the doorway. She is an upper-class woman, also from Ireland. She is wearing an expensive men's bathrobe over a pair of plain pajamas. A survivor of polio, Evie uses a cane and walks with difficulty. Her left arm is partially paralyzed, as is one of her legs. She crosses aggressively into the room, brandishing a poker while maneuvering with her cane. A survivor of extraordinary losses and suffering early in life, EVIE is a no-nonsense, can-do, take-charge kind of woman.)* Where are you? Come out! Come out! *(She notices the wide-open window and crosses to it, looking out.)* Out the window, is it? Well! *(She closes it firmly and locks it. She turns to face MAINIE.)* So… *(MAINIE hasn't moved.)* Who is he?

MAINIE: *(Dazed.)* Who?

EVIE: The man… the thief… *(MAINIE looks blankly at her.)* There was *someone* in your room…?

MAINIE: No…

EVIE: An intruder…?

MAINIE: No…

EVIE: *(A beat.)* I heard a scream…?

MAINIE: Oh, that was me. *(Silence. EVIE scans the room again. This time she notices the turpentine and the broken cup on the floor. She picks it up and sniffs it.)*

EVIE: Did you drink that?

MAINIE: *(Frightened.)* What?

EVIE: *(Grabbing her arm and pointing to the liquid on the floor.) Did you drink the turpentine? (A beat.) Tell me! Did you drink it? (Another beat.)* Right. To hospital then! *(Pulling MAINIE.)*

MAINIE: No! No, I didn't! *(EVIE moves in to smell her breath.)* I was going to, but I didn't… I swear.

EVIE: *(Releasing her arm.)* Well… Let's clean it up then, shall we? *(Pushing up her sleeves, she crosses to the wash basin.)*

MAINIE: No, no… I can do it. Please… Go back to bed.

EVIE: And wait for you to light a cigarette and incinerate the entire rooming house and half of London? I think not. Bad enough to sit up most the night waiting for air raid sirens and wondering if we'll all be bombed to bits by morning… I don't want to fancy myself waking up in a bloody crematorium… *(Retrieving an expensive towel.)* This is going to ruin your towel.

MAINIE: *(Finally moving, she crosses to EVIE and takes the towel.)* It's all right. I can clean it.

EVIE: Yes, I'm sure you *can*, but the question is "*Will you?*"

MAINIE: *(Bristling.)* I told you I would… I'm *fine*.

EVIE: Oh, yes, screaming like a banshee in the middle of the night, the window wide open for any hooligan in London, and topping it off with a nightcap of paint thinner!

MAINIE: I didn't drink it!

EVIE: But you were going to.

MAINIE: But I didn't.

EVIE: *(Shaking her head.)* I have some rags in my room. And get that nightgown off. Turpentine is absorbed through the skin. You'll have a nasty burn. *(She exits, taking the poker with her. MAINIE turns to look at the room. Slowly, she pulls the cloth cover back over her canvas and picks up the crumpled papers and puts them into the trash bin. She pulls the blanket up on her bed and sits woodenly. EVIE returns with a basin and some clean rags. She also has a bottle of brandy under her arm.)* I told you to take off your nightgown. It's soaked in turpentine.

MAINIE: Oh…

EVIE: *(Pulling off her robe.)* Here. You can put this on. I'm afraid your gown is quite ruined. *(EVIE, with some difficulty gets down on the floor and begins to scrub. MAINIE crosses behind the screen and slips out of the nightgown and into the robe. EVIE glances up.)* And sponge off your chest. It's going to burn. *(MAINIE crosses tentatively to the basin and sponges her chest under the robe. EVIE doesn't look up.)*

MAINIE: I'm Mainie Jellett.

EVIE: *(Not looking up.)* I know who you are.

MAINIE: I'm a student at the Westminster School of Art.

EVIE: *(Still not looking up.)* So am I.

MAINIE: But I don't recognize you…

EVIE: Well, that's to be expected.

MAINIE: Why?

EVIE: *(Matter-of-fact.)* Because you are the most popular girl in the school and because I walk with a limp.

MAINIE: *(Annoyed.)* And what does that have to do with it? *(EVIE shakes her head without looking at her.)* That has nothing to do with it!

EVIE: No, of course not. It never does.

MAINIE: *(Uncomfortable.)* Are you going to tell me your name?

EVIE: *(A beat.)* Evie Hone.

MAINIE: I *do* know it! Evie Hone! You're the new student. They said there was someone coming in September... See, I *do* know you... I just didn't know it was *you*. And you've only just gotten here... *(EVIE gives her a look.) And* you're from Dublin. *(She watches EVIE for a moment.)* I'm a Dubliner, too.

EVIE: Where?

MAINIE: Fitzwilliam Square. My father is a barrister... Queen's Counsel. *(EVIE is still scrubbing.)* Where are *you* from?

EVIE: *(Finishing up.)* Well, when? I've been living here in London for the last three years, but before that I was touring in Spain and Italy, and before that I was studying in Switzerland...

MAINIE: I mean, where did you grow up?

EVIE: Dublin. Roebuck Grove.

MAINIE: The estate?

EVIE: *(Smiling.)* My father was a Governor of the Bank of Ireland.

MAINIE: *(Impressed.)* Oh. *(A beat.)* What does he do now?

EVIE: Nothing. He's dead. So's my mother.

MAINIE: I'm sorry.

EVIE: Well, I never knew her. She died the day I was born. Are you feeling better?

MAINIE: Yes, thank you. *(EVIE gets up from the floor.)*

EVIE: I'm afraid it's going to be a bit whiffy for a while. *(EVIE starts to cross toward the door with the basin.)*

MAINIE: Wait…! Please don't go!

EVIE: I wasn't going to. I just wanted to set the rags outside the door. *(She puts the basin with rags outside the door and closes it.)* I brought us some brandy.

MAINIE: Oh...

EVIE: It's Armagnac. Have you ever had it?

MAINIE: No…

EVIE: *(Occupied with opening the bottle.)* Armagnac is from Gascony. The oldest brandy distilled in France… introduced by the Moors in the 14th century. *(She has opened the bottle and looks expectantly at MAINIE.)*

MAINIE: Oh… I'm afraid that all I have is teacups. *(A beat. She takes two cups from a shelf.)*

EVIE: It was originally consumed for therapeutic benefits. Armagnac was believed to cure hepatitis, gout, fistula… *(Pouring.)* And... paralysis. *(She looks up and smiles.)* Apparently not. *(An awkward pause. EVIE moves close to MAINIE.)* Armagnac is more forceful, more complicated than cognac… even excessive sometimes. *(She lifts the cup and takes a sip. MAINIE follows suit.)* Well?

MAINIE: *(Responding to EVIE's proximity.)* I like it.

EVIE: Fire and earth.

MAINIE: Fire and earth! *(She lifts the cup again for a second taste.)*

EVIE: So…?

MAINIE: *(Smiling seductively.)* So… ?

EVIE: Why were you screaming and drinking turpentine?

MAINIE: *(Piqued.)* I told you I *didn't* drink it. *(A beat.)* I had a dream. *(A beat.)* A nightmare, actually. It was so vivid, it woke me up. It was so realistic, I was afraid it might be true. *(She looks at EVIE.)* Well… it seems rather silly now.

EVIE: What was the dream?

MAINIE: *(Very reluctant.)* Oh… no, I… I don't—

EVIE: I believe I've earned the right to hear it.

MAINIE: *(After a moment.)* Well... It was about Professor Sickert. Do you know him?

EVIE: I'm in his life painting class.

MAINIE: So am I!

EVIE: Yes, I know. *(MAINIE is embarrassed again.)* So, you had a dream about Walter Sickert?

MAINIE: Do you like him?

EVIE: The man has never spoken a word to me.

MAINIE: Fortunate for you… He told me my painting was vacuous… that I was "obsessed with cliché."

EVIE: *(Laughing.)* "Obsessed with cliché…?"

MAINIE: He said that I was "intellectually bankrupt," and that my painting was the outcome of decades of artistic inbreeding—and that all I could paint was obscene monster!

EVIE: *(Rising and crossing to the easel.)* Really? He said that…? What a stupid, little man. *(Pausing in front of the covered easel.)* May I…? *(MAINIE doesn't say anything. EVIE holds up a corner of the sheet and studies it. MAINIE watches for her reaction. EVIE smiles dismissively.)* "Female nude seated."

MAINIE: *(Piqued.)* That's all?

EVIE: What do you want me to say?

MAINIE: Tell me the truth.

EVIE: Oh, I think not.

MAINIE: Why?

EVIE: The truth is only for very good friends, and I don't have any. *(A beat.)* Tell me about your dream.

MAINIE: Oh, that's only for very good friends, and you're not one.

EVIE: Fair enough. Well, then, if you tell me your dream, I will tell you what I think of your painting. *(Dropping the corner of the sheet back over the painting.)* Have we got a deal?

MAINIE: *(She considers before speaking.)* Before I tell you the dream, I should tell you about something that happened. *(A beat.)* Professor Sickert asked me if I would like to see some *real* paintings—paintings that were "pages torn from the book of life."

EVIE: "Torn from the book of life?" *(Laughing.)* Well, *that's* not cliché at all!

MAINIE: *(Grim.)* Actually, he wanted me to accompany him to his studio. *(EVIE stops laughing. Long silence. MAINIE looks at the floor.)*

EVIE: This wasn't the dream…?

MAINIE: No. This really happened. *(Another silence.)* At first, I told him I couldn't… Unless, of course, he wanted to invite the rest of the class… but then he became very angry and he told me this was my obsession with cliché… and that he didn't really understand why I had come to Westminster at all if I was unwilling to learn, unwilling to go through the same rigors as male painters. *(Imitating Sickert.)* How could women expect to paint, to sculpt like Michaelangelo, Botticelli… if we are too squeamish to work with male models, if we insist on the presence of a chaperone for every visit to an artist's studio…?

EVIE: So Walter resents having females in his class, does he? A pity the war is butchering all his aspiring Michaelangelos.

MAINIE: I thought his studio would be in Camden, near the art school. That I would be able to walk back…

EVIE: *(Pouring herself more brandy.)* But of course, it wasn't.

MAINIE: It was in Whitechapel.

EVIE: Oh, dear god.

MAINIE: *(Defensively.)* I didn't know! He had hired a car… and by the time I realized where we were going, it was too late. The car stopped on this horrid little street in front of this appalling structure… some sort of squalid lodging house.

EVIE: You didn't go in…

MAINIE: You're going to think I am a complete ninny...

EVIE: No. *(A beat.)* Not at all.

MAINIE: I didn't feel I could say no. I didn't know where I was. I didn't want to be alone in Whitechapel. And the cabbie… the way he was looking at me… I didn't know what else to do. *(MAINIE has become visibly distressed.)*

EVIE: Walter must have been enjoying the situation immensely.

MAINIE: I don't know. *(Long silence. EVIE pours MAINIE some more Armagnac.)*

EVIE: *(Toasting.)* "Long life…"

MAINIE: *(Distracted, she responds automatically finishing the phrase of the Irish toast.)* "… and a merry one." *(She clinks the cups and starts to drink, but EVIE intercepts to finish her toast.)*

EVIE: "A quick death…"

MAINIE: *(Shocked.)* What?

EVIE: The second half of the toast…? "A quick death…" *(EVIE waits, but MAINIE is silent. EVIE finishes the toast herself.)* "And an easy one." *(EVIE drinks; MAINIE doesn't.)*

MAINIE: He had a studio. It was an actual studio…

EVIE: Of course it was. Hideous man. *(Long pause.)* Go on.

MAINIE: *(Setting down her cup.)* Actually, I'm not used to people who don't like me.

EVIE: *(Smiling.)* Ah, the very definition of "most popular girl."

MAINIE: Why? Why don't you like me? What have I done?

EVIE: What have you done? *(Smiling.)* Well… You have needed to ask that question. *(There is a long silence.)* "He had a studio…"

MAINIE: *(A beat.)* Yes. I followed him up these broken stairs, and down this filthy hall, and he took out a key and opened a door. And there was a bed… I remember it had an iron bedstead. He saw me take a step back and said, "It's for the models. I paint them on the bed." He had this revolting smile on his face. I'd never seen him look like that in class. I'd never seen him smile. In fact, he appeared to have become another person entirely.

EVIE: *(A nod.)* Ah.

MAINIE: You've seen him change like that?

EVIE: No. But I am quite familiar with the Dr.-Jekyll-and-Mr.-Hyde metamorphosis. Did you go in?

MAINIE: No. I just stood there. I couldn't move. He brought out some paintings to show me... I think he wanted to prove that he painted the models lying on the bed.

EVIE: And were they cliché?

MAINIE: They were absolutely the ugliest, the most grotesque, the most vile things I have ever seen!

EVIE: Nudes?

MAINIE: They were more like cadavers... cadavers that had been left in the sun! The women's bodies were purple and yellow, and you couldn't see their faces... they were all blurry. Meat! That's what they were... the women were carrion! And there were men in the pictures, men with all their clothes on, sitting on the bed or hovering over the naked women. And I said, "I want to go back." And he laughed at me. He said, "You've come all this way, and now you don't even want to see the rest of my paintings?" He was mocking me.

EVIE: He was manipulating you.

MAINIE: I just stood there in the hall.

EVIE: Good for you.

MAINIE: He asked me if I thought Jack the Ripper might have lived there. I didn't say anything, and he asked me if I knew who Jack the Ripper was. And then he said that it was rumored that the murderer lived in this neighborhood, and that—*(Imitating Sickert.)* *"—who knows?—perhaps this was his very room… imagine… Jack the Ripper's room!"* Then he said I had nothing to fear, because the Ripper only murdered prostitutes—women who "deserved it."

EVIE: Swine.

MAINIE: I was terrified.

EVIE: And with every reason.

MAINIE: I felt like my feet were welded to the floor. I couldn't move. It was as if we were in a painting ourselves… Frozen in time. I don't know how long it lasted—him standing by that open door and me standing in the hall. As if we had stood like that for centuries… And I feel as if some part of me is standing there still, waiting for something inevitable and terrifying to happen.

EVIE: *(Smacking the cork back in the bottle of Armagnac with finality.)* It already happened.

MAINIE: Yes! That's the thing! Something already happened. Something terrible… And then we walked back down the stairs… he was behind me the whole time … I could feel him mocking me with his eyes… It was as if I was his little dog and he was taking me out on a leash! *(A beat.)* We got in the car back to Westminster, and the whole time, he ignored me completely, talking with the cabbie, who kept turning around and leering at me.

EVIE: And yet you still attend his class…?

MAINIE: I don't know how not to. *(EVIE looks at her.)* I mean, nothing really happened. He invited me to his studio and showed me his paintings. *(She bursts into tears. EVIE rises abruptly and begins to pace. EVIE crosses to the canvas and uncovers it again. She stands in front of it. MAINIE, still weeping, looks up.) That* was in the dream.

EVIE: What was?

MAINIE: "Female Nude Seated." That was the part that made me scream…

EVIE: *(Studying the canvas.)* Well, I admit, it's a bit pedestrian, but I hardly think screaming—

MAINIE: *(Cutting her off.)* You think this is funny!

EVIE: *(Serious and angry.)* I think *everything* is funny. Funny as a crutch. *(A beat.)* Do go on.

MAINIE: *(Long pause.)* The dream started out in Sickert's life painting class. The model walks in—that model… *(Indicating the painting.)* And she's wrapped in that same blue sheet… and Professor Sickert is escorting her up to the model's chair at the front of the class, and when he turns around, he has that smile on his face…

EVIE: Ah... the "Mr. Hyde" face.

MAINIE: And then the model sits down on the chair—that chair *(Again, indicating the painting.)* And she looks like she's about to say something… But when she opens her mouth, it's filled with blood that starts pouring out… and then her head falls back, and her throat has been slashed… It's nearly cut through her neck… and *then* Sickert picks up a corner of the blue sheet and pulls it open… and there is this great gash all the way from her sternum to her pelvis, and suddenly her intestines start spilling out over her thighs… And I turn to the other students, but they're all staring at their canvases, busy painting… and then I turn back to my easel, and I see that I have painted her, too… just the way she looks… disemboweled… And then Sickert is standing over my shoulder looking at the canvas, which, by this time, is dripping with blood, and he is laughing at me. *(She stops abruptly.)*

EVIE: Well, that would make me scream.

MAINIE: The dream was so real, I was afraid it was true. I had to get up and look at the canvas. *(A beat.)* I feel as if I am going mad.

EVIE: Indeed. You and half of London.

MAINIE: What do you mean?

EVIE: What have you got to eat? *(She has begun to rummage briskly among the shelves.)* Ah, biscuits…! *(She retrieves the tin.)* Huntley and Palmers… Excellent. May I…?

MAINIE: What do you mean, half of London is going mad?

EVIE: *(Reading the label.)* You know they're manufacturing these with honey now instead of sugar… Bloody war rations… Last week I was in Victoria Tower Gardens, and would you believe the police have actually started handing citations to people for feeding the pigeons!

MAINIE: Who else is going mad?

EVIE: Other than the pigeons and the police…? *(She bites into a cookie.)* Well, there are the boys who were at the Somme—the ones unfortunate enough to make it back. And the boys who are now at Passchendaele, if they haven't already suffocated in the mud. And their mothers. And their sisters. And their aunties. And their sweethearts. Swarms of frantic women dashing to the railway station to collect their returning heroes—to press their darling boys to their breasts again… the nightmare finally over! *(Dramatizing.)* But they can't make sense of it…! Here they are, at the very station, at the very hour designated in the telegram… but yet, no son, no brother, no nephew, no sweetheart! The train has come and gone, the passengers have all met their various parties and dispersed… but there is no one left… oh, except some dreadful, crippled, blind boy leaning against the stationhouse wall, slumped over a crutch—his leg amputated and his nose missing from his face, but never mind. This cannot be their son, their brother, their nephew, their sweetheart. Half of London is waking from a hideous nightmare and lifting the cover on the canvas, only to discover that it hasn't been a dream at all… but of course, it's not polite to scream.

MAINIE: *(Long silence.)* Do you think Walter Sickert is Jack the Ripper?

EVIE: What I think doesn't matter. What I *know* is that he admires the man, and that, if he isn't the Ripper, he wishes he was, and, in the realm of the spirit, that is the same thing. What I *know* is that Walter Sickert has raped your psyche. *(EVIE finishes her brandy and looks at MAINIE. MAINIE crosses the room. She stands in front of her easel and uncovers it.)*

MAINIE: Well, that was the dream. Now, you have to tell me what you think of my painting.

EVIE: *(Without looking.)* The most popular girl paints the most beautiful girl. Theme and variation.

MAINIE: *(Angry.)* Oh, and what about when the *unpopular* girl paints the *ugly* girl? What do you call that?

EVIE: Well... *(With disarming candor.)* I call that a self-portrait. *(A long pause. EVIE rises briskly.)* Well... I leave you to the Armagnac and the honey biscuits—*(As EVIE maneuvers toward the door, MAINIE suddenly crosses in front of her and kisses her. It's a long kiss that engages both of them fully. MAINIE takes a step back.)*

MAINIE: *(Suggestively.)* I have your robe.

EVIE: It's yours.

MAINIE: Stay.

EVIE: *(Touching MAINIE's hair.)* I should tell you something.

MAINIE: Oh, no… no, no, no don't! Please don't!

EVIE: I am leaving Westminster.

MAINIE: But you only just arrived!

EVIE: I'm joining a convent.

MAINIE: *(Angry.)* Well, that's original!

EVIE: The Convent of the Epiphany. In Cornwall. It's an Anglican sisterhood.

MAINIE: *(A long silence as MAINIE absorbs this.)* But why?

EVIE: *(Still touching her hair.)* Because I need to be with women.

MAINIE: You are with one tonight.

EVIE: Yes. *(EVIE kisses her. Suddenly MAINIE breaks away.)*

MAINIE: But what about your art…? Are you just going to abandon that?

EVIE: "Female nude seated…?"

MAINIE: But you don't have to paint that!

EVIE: *(Smiling.)* Landscapes? Portraits…? Birds?

MAINIE: *(Venting.)* No! No! That's the problem!

EVIE: Problem?

MAINIE: *(Passionate.)* Why does every picture have to tell a story? Why can't art be as pure as music? Must it always be tainted by some form of voyeurism? Isn't it possible to create a painting that is as spiritual as music?

EVIE: A song to the eye?

MAINIE: Yes! Exactly! A song to the eye… Something that is more than a… a… *reminiscence* of life—something that *lives* on its own! Life! I want to create paintings that pull the viewer into movement with them… instead of forcing them to be a voyeur! When *I* paint a woman, I want it to be something that is impossible for men to appropriate for their fantasies and their fetishes! Art should be an expression of spirituality!

EVIE: *(Smiling.)* Perhaps *you* should join a convent.

MAINIE: *(Angry.)* A prison! It would be a prison… living in a *literal* cell, never being allowed to leave without permission! Every minute of every day regimented… I don't understand how you can be so willing to give up your freedom!

EVIE: But I'm not. I'll be gaining it.

MAINIE: How can you say that?

EVIE: Actually Plotinus said it… Do you read the Greeks? *(MAINIE stares at her.)* Well, he wrote that there are three types of humans—First, those who live materially, like birds who are too heavy for their wings and can't fly at all. And then there are those who can only fly a little bit above the earth—just enough to catch a glimpse of possibilities… but they aren't strong enough, and they end up falling back on the very conditions they had hoped to escape. And then, finally, Plotinus names the third type. These are the godlike ones who have a clear vision of the higher truths, who live in the realm of spirit above the "fog and cloud of earth…" He describes such a person as one who is *"returning after long wanderings to the pleasant ways of his own country."* So, you see, I shall be going home.

MAINIE: *(Stunned, after a moment.)* Well, I think that's the most selfish thing I ever heard! To just go off—to *fly* off—to some private little kingdom of contemplative bliss, leaving everyone and everything behind... hoarding your happiness all for yourself, not even attempting to share it with the rest of us... *flightless, lumbering dodo birds*!

EVIE: From the girl who drinks turpentine.

MAINIE: I didn't drink it! I was only *considering* drinking it! And you don't know anything about me or about my life! You don't know anything about anything! And did it ever occur to you that my popularity, which seems to be such a source of envy for you... did it ever occur to you that it might come at a very high price? That the second I stop being pleasing to people, it will all just evaporate like water? You don't know anything about anything! You don't understand *anything* about what happened tonight!

EVIE: *(Stung deeply.)* Clearly. *(She turns to go.)*

MAINIE: Oh, don't you dare! Don't you dare go out that door, Evie Hone! You have barged in here, because you needed someone to rescue, and then you have painted me as a spoiled, ignorant, narcissistic, silly, little girl! And now that you are done with your noble mission, you think you can just stack your little canvas over in the corner with all your other studies of people who failed to measure up to your vast experience of life and your exalted spiritual vision! If you walk out, you take that nasty caricature with you! Don't you dare leave it here, because it's not mine! It's not who I am! It's a portrait of your own arrogance! Take it with you!

EVIE: And what about your image of me?

MAINIE: Oh, it's accurate!

EVIE: Not, it's not! It's cliché! *(She begins goading MAINIE.)* It's storytelling! It's the work of a cheap voyeur!

MAINIE: Get out!

EVIE: *(Not moving. There is a standoff.)* Why don't you test your theories tonight?

MAINIE: What do you mean?

EVIE: Paint me!

MAINIE: Why should I?

EVIE: Because I am the perfect subject for your study. Paint a female nude who has survived polio, quarantined away for years in hospital wards. Paint a female nude who has wasted her childhood in bed, encased in a plaster-of-paris straitjacket, her legs shackled to splints. Paint a female nude whose limbs are deformed by disease and disfigured by the butchery from a hundred worthless surgeries. Paint a female nude whose body has been the object of curiosity and experiment by scores of doctors, fetishized by professional men who by day pose as the saints who dedicate their lives to relieving the suffering of afflicted children, and who, by night, raid the wards for victims too immobilized to resist, too young to understand, too isolated to be rescued, and too traumatized to remember!

MAINIE: *(Long pause. Slowly, MAINIE crosses to her easel. She removes the canvas of the nude, replacing it with a fresh one. She moves the easel to face toward the wingback chair, at an angle where the audience cannot see the canvas. The chair faces away from the audience. MAINIE takes the sheet that was used to cover the canvas to create a drape over the chair. [This will prevent the audience from seeing EVIE's bare legs.] EVIE rises and, with her back to the audience, removes her pajama shirt. Seated in the chair, she removes her pajama bottoms. MAINIE glances briefly at EVIE's legs. She reaches for her charcoal and begins to sketch.)* Were you in Dublin last summer?

EVIE: *(Distracted.)* What?

MAINIE: Last summer… Were you in Ireland?

EVIE: I told you, I've been living in London for three years.

MAINIE: *(MAINIE continues to sketch through this conversation.)* I was home in Dublin in June. That was when they released the prisoners from the Easter Rebellion.

EVIE: I read about it in the *Times.*

MAINIE: They put them all on a boat at Holyhead, and then, when they got to Dublin Port, they put them on a train to Westland Row Station. I went to see them… Are you comfortable?

EVIE: Never. Go on.

MAINIE: My family, of course, didn't know where I was going… I walked from Fitzwilliam Square, because the station was only a half mile from my home. But I couldn't have hired a car anyway, the streets were so crowded. It took me an hour to get to the train. There were thousands and thousands of people. I'd never seen crowds like that in my life… Are you cold?

EVIE: Not yet.

MAINIE: And then, when I got to the station, I heard that the prisoners had already disembarked, and that there was a parade forming, but I couldn't get close enough to see it. There was a band somewhere and it was playing "A Nation Once Again." Everyone started singing—everyone… the men in topcoats, the laborers, the schoolchildren, the women with their babies, the girls waving their green handkerchiefs.

EVIE: Were you surprised?

MAINIE: *(Pausing to consider the question.)* Was I surprised? I have lived my entire life in Dublin, and I never really saw it until that moment. *(She pauses.)* I looked up and there was a woman above the heads of the crowd. She was dressed in black and standing tall like a statue. She began moving forward slowly, as if she were an icon being carried in a religious procession… It was Countess Markievicz. She must have been standing in an open motor car… just standing—not smiling, not waving—just standing like the masthead of some enormous ship, parting the humanity of Great Brunswick Street. And I felt this overwhelming urge to kneel on the pavement. The crowd was pressing forward to follow her, but I couldn't move. Tears were running down my face. People began pushing past me, hundreds and hundreds of them, but I couldn't move.

EVIE: *(Nodding.)* You were on sacred ground.

MAINIE: Well, I never felt anything like that in a church. I kept thinking about how, after her arrest, the Countess had to listen to the executions of her comrades, as they took them out, one-by-one, day-after-day, and shot them in the prison courtyard.

EVIE: Quite a woman.

MAINIE: My father calls her a coward and a traitor. He says, sex be damned, they should have shot her with the others.

EVIE: I believe she requested it.

MAINIE: I couldn't go home after the parade. I walked down to the river and then over to the General Post Office. I hadn't seen the GPO since the British shelled it a year ago. I think I had been afraid to see it. But it was just an empty facade… not frightening at all. The pillars, the portico, the statues, all perfectly intact… but the entire building behind it was gone… just rubble. Standing before it, I could see the clouds passing behind the windows. It was oddly peaceful, like a gateway or a picture frame to an unconquered country. And then I walked to St. Stephen's Green, where the Countess had fought and where she had surrendered. And I kept thinking how everything was different and yet the same… how the grass and the leaves were shimmering and radiant. It was like a dream... except that the Dublin of my childhood was the dream, and that this Dublin, now, was real. I was being initiated into a world of spirit underneath the skin of the city… behind the facade. And in that initiation, I was having the same experience of shimmering and radiance. I sat there I the park until the sun set, experiencing this intense happiness… I can't describe it. It was like being part of something magnificent. I didn't want to go home. *(Setting down the charcoal and dusting her hands.)* In a sense, I have never been home again.

EVIE: Why are you telling me this?

MAINIE: Because you want to go to a convent, when there is a resurrection happening in Ireland. It is the living thing itself, and not just a reminiscence.

EVIE: What about you?

MAINIE: No. I can't go back. I can't go home.

EVIE: And does this have anything to do with the papers that were all over the floor when I entered, but which have since so mysteriously vanished?

MAINIE: *(A beat. MAINIE crosses to the trash bin and pulls out the papers. She hands them to EVIE, who, still seated, has wrapped the sheet around herself.)* Here…

EVIE: *(Examining them.)* Ah. Letters to your father…

MAINIE: He's running for Parliament next year, to put down the rebellion.

EVIE: *(Turning them over.)* But they are all unfinished…?.

MAINIE: Yes. Theme and variation… *(Abruptly, she picks up the canvas.)* Every thing I attempt is unfinished.

EVIE: Wait! May I see? *(EVIE takes the canvas.)* But you didn't paint my legs…

MAINIE: Yes, I did.

EVIE: It's just geometric shapes.

MAINIE: Well then, you see, I failed. *(She tries to take the canvas from EVIE, but EVIE does not relinquish it.)*

EVIE: No, wait. *(She studies the canvas in silence.)*

MAINIE: I was thinking about the GPO.

EVIE: My legs and the Post Office?

MAINIE: I was remembering the sensation I felt when I saw the clouds through the windows of the bombed-out GPO, and I could only see them, because the structure behind the façade had been destroyed. And the clouds, the sky had never appeared so brilliant, so vivid as they did through those windows. The absence of the edifice had created a negative space that made possible this extraordinary vision of what is usually obscured. *(EVIE is watching MAINIE, as she explains her canvas.)* And what I was trying to do here...*(MAINIE points to something on the canvas)*...with these planes—I was attepting to create a kind of tension.

EVIE: Tension?

MAINIE: *(Exploding with emotion.)* Oh my god, Evie... So much tension! You have this incredible vulnerability, and at the same time, this phenomenal strength... And all these sharp edges and angles, but they aren't dissonant, because there is this amazing courage that holds it all together, in this dynamic balance. I wanted to show that wholeness, that perfection.

EVIE: *(Deeply moved.)* You know it's only failure if you quit.

MAINIE: *(Deflated, she takes the canvas.)* Well... there we are.

EVIE: I tell you what... I will make a deal with you. I will give up my plan to enter the convent, if you will finish the painting… But you have to promise to leave Westminster. You have to promise you will go where there are teachers who can understand what you are trying to do, who can help you create your "art as pure as music."

MAINIE: *(Excited.)* Paris! They are in Paris—the artists who are painting in a new way. They're not afraid to break the tradition. Oh, Evie… what they are doing in Paris—

EVIE: Well, then, that is where you must go! *(MAINIE, turns away with a laugh.)* Why not?

MAINIE: My family… They won't understand. They *can't* understand.

EVIE: Then you must find a new family.

MAINIE: *(Long silence.)* Would you come with me? *(EVIE hesitates.)* You said you wanted to be with women… What about a community of women artists? Evie, let's make one! In Paris… In Ireland! I know how to do that! I do! I'm the most popular girl, remember?

EVIE: How could I forget? *(As the women embrace, EVIE's sheet begins to slip to the floor. Blackout.)*

End of Play

52 Pickup

A Ten-Minute Play

Cast of Characters

JANIYA: A woman, any age.

CIL: Janiya's ex.

Scene
Patient's room on a psych ward or in a psych hospital.

Time
The present.

52 Pickup

Lights come up on a hospital room. JANIYA has been committed on a mandatory suicide watch. She is wearing paper scrubs. Bored, she thumbs through a magazine. There is a knock on the door.

JANIYA: *(Dropping the magazine, she looks up.)* Carly… ? Is that you…? Carly?

CIL: *(Offstage.)* Not Carly. *(Long silence. JANIYA picks up her magazine.)* Can I come in? *(Silence.)* Okay. I'm comin' in. *(CIL enters. She is carrying a small paper bag.)*

JANIYA: *(Not looking up.)* I didn't say you could come in.

CIL: You didn't say I couldn't.

JANIYA: *(Lowering the paper.)* I thought you were Carly.

CIL: Yeah, I heard that. You just be glad anybody came to see you. *(JANIYA picks up her magazine again.)* You're not really expecting your girlfriend to come see you after what you just did? *(Pause.)* What you just did for the *third* time…?

JANIYA: *(Tossing the magazine to the side.)* I'm in a hospital. That's what girlfriends are supposed to do… They come see their partners when they're in the hospital.

CIL: And how many times you expect them to do that. *(JANIYA doesn't say anything.)* Yeah. And, you didn't have to go and get yourself locked up.

JANIYA: Yes, I did.

CIL: They asked you in the ER, after you woke up, if you were going to try to kill yourself again and you said you were thinking about it.

JANIYA: *Thinking* about it.

CIL: Well, you know they gotta lock you up when you say shit like that. You know that and don't act like you don't. I know you, Janiya… Remember? You used to live with me.

JANIYA: I *was* thinking about it.

CIL: Well, if you don't want to be here, the next time they ask you that, just lie. And don't act like you don't know how to do that. You lied all the time with me.

JANIYA: No I didn't.

CIL: There you go.

JANIYA: Not all the time.

CIL: I asked you if you were seeing Carly and you said no.

JANIYA: I didn't want to hurt you.

CIL: No, you just wanted to keep your options open before you made up your mind. And what makes you think Carly would want to come see you?

JANIYA: Well, you did.

CIL: That's because you already left me. I had two years to get over that. Carly, she's just learning.

JANIYA: You're not making me feel any better.

CIL: Yeah, well, you're not making any of us feel better either, so we're even.

JANIYA: Is that why you came here? To make me feel bad?

CIL: Yeah, that's why I came here. That's why I went to the store and got you some candy bars and some smoked almonds and a deck of cards. To make you feel bad. *(She hands her the bag.)*

JANIYA: Thanks. *(She goes through the candy bars.)* Oh, yeah… You remember what I like.

CIL: I'm good like that.

JANIYA: So who told you?

CIL: Carly did. *(JANIYA looks up, surprised.)* Yeah. Right after the ambulance came. Called me first. You going to get some help here?

JANIYA: Here? No. They send a doctor in to see you. That's all.

CIL: Has she seen you?

JANIYA: Yeah.

CIL: What's she say?

JANIYA: She said it was PTSD. I coulda told her that.

CIL: She give you pills?

JANIYA: Not this time. Put me down for "cognitive-something therapy." Reframe my negative thinking….

CIL: Good luck with that.

JANIYA: I don't have negative thoughts. *(She opens the deck.)*

CIL: Third time you've tried to kill yourself in six months and you don't have negative thoughts? *(Pause.)* Well, if you don't, I sure as hell do.

JANIYA: Come on, let's play… *(She holds the deck out for CIL to cut. CIL cuts.)*

CIL: So you don't have negative thoughts?

JANIYA: No.

CIL: You have positive thoughts…?

JANIYA: I have positive thoughts.

CIL: Like what?

JANIYA: Like "I'm not stupid enough to keep sitting at the table when I got dealt a shit hand and everyone else is playing with a marked deck."

CIL: *(Laying down her hand.)* What's that bad hand, Janiya? A girlfriend who loves you? Your health? What? Your job? What's that bad hand that's so awful you wanna quit?

JANIYA: What happened to me as a kid.

CIL: But that was then.

JANIYA: No, that is now, because I can't sleep without waking up and I keep getting these memories right in the middle of work. I'll be helping some customer and bam… suddenly I hear a door slam… and I'm having a panic attack so bad they have to send me home. I can't keep my job, and that means I can't pay the rent, and Carly's going to kick me out… So I'll have to go live in some homeless shelter… won't be able to take my cat. And I wont have any of my stuff… I'll have to sell my car—

CIL: Okay, okay, okay. The bad hand. I get it. *(Pause.)* If that happens, you can move in with me.

JANIYA: Oh, yeah. That would be great.

CIL: What?

JANIYA: Fuckin' charity case.

CIL: Friend helping out a friend.

JANIYA: Charity case.

CIL: *(Really angry.)* Fuck you. *(JANIYA shrugs.)* Fuck you and your bad hand. Oh, look—I got one, too…! *(She throws her hand at JANIYA, and then she picks up the rest of the deck and throws that up in the air. It lands all over the floor. There is a moment of silence, and suddenly JANIYA bursts out laughing.)*

JANIYA: Yeah! That's what I'm talking about!

CIL: What?

JANIYA: Didn't that feel good? Tell the truth, Cil. Didn't that feel good? You sittin' there tryin' so hard to get me to say something you want to hear, and me not sayin' it no matter what… And you just tryin' harder and harder… and then you just be like "Fuck it! Just take the whole game and just 'fuck it!'" Didn't that feel good?

CIL: *(Considering.)* Yeah… I guess it did.

JANIYA: Well…?

CIL: Well, what?

JANIYA: Well, that's what it's like. That's what it's like taking that whole bottle of pills. That's just what it's like. Just fuck this shit. Fuck this game I can't win. Whole new game…

CIL: It's not a game.

JANIYA: Yeah, it is. "52 Pickup." That's what it is.

CIL: 52 Pickup is a joke. It's not a game.

JANIYA: Oh, yeah it is. It's a game on my terms. Suicide is 52 Pickup. *(There's a long silence.)*

CIL: Okay. But if that's true, then you can't even play your own game.

JANIYA: What do you mean?

CIL: Well it's not "52 Fuck Shit Up." It's "52 Pickup." Like the cards have to get picked up. You don't stick around for that when you kill yourself. There's Carly coming home from work, all "honey-I'm-home…" and then that silence. And your car in the driveway, and you've already tried twice… and so that's messing with her head right there, like a horror movie… So then she goes to the bedroom… and she has to open that door and wonder if you're in there. And you are, and then she has to wonder if you're sleeping or not. And so she has to yell at you and shake you… so now she knows you're not sleeping, so she has to figure out if you're dead or in a coma or some shit… so now she has to take your pulse—

JANIYA: *(Cutting her off.)* Is this supposed to help me with my positive thinking?

CIL: *(Escalating.)* No, this is the game, the damn game. *Your 52 Damn Pickup.* This is the pickup part. Yeah… and so then the ambulance comes and she has to watch them do all that stuff with you…

JANIYA: Okay, okay. I get it.

CIL: Yeah. Well… so, it's your turn.

JANIYA: What's my turn?

CIL: I threw the fifty-two. Your turn to do the pickup. Go on. Cause I'm *here* for this damn game. I am *so* here for this motherfucking game. Go on. Get your fuckin' ass off this bed and pick up those goddam cards. Pick 'em up! *(Screaming.)* Goddam it, you fuckin' pick up those goddam, motherfuckin' cards! *(Frightened, JANIYA gets off the bed and onto the floor. She starts to pick up the cards.)* And I'm gonna count 'em and they better all be there. All fifty-two of them. Because that's how you play… I throw the cards and *you* clean 'em up. *(JANIYA turns to her.)* No, goddam it! You pick 'em up! Because that's the game. That's the game you want to play…? You fuckin' play it! *You* pick 'em up now…! There's one over there…

JANIYA: I'm sorry…

CIL: Oh, yeah, that's the game, too. You don't think Carly's sorry? You don't think I'm sorry? You don't think all the ambulance people and all the doctors and all the nurses out here… you don't think they're sorry? Oh, trust me, all of us picking up your shit for you…? Yeah, we are sorry. So *you* be feelin' sorry now. That's the game. *(JANIYA, still on the floor, starts to cry.)* Yeah. You cry. Carly's cryin'. I'm too pissed to cry, but I have, I will. Oh, I will. That's the picking up. *(Long silence as JANIYA sobs. JANIYA is really crying, like a baby.)* Oh, shit. Girl, you can't even play cards. *(CIL gets on the floor with her and begins to pick up the cards.)* Here… here… Count 'em. *(She hands the cards to JANIYA, who remains unresponsive, given over to her sobbing.)* Damn. *(More crying.)* Goddam it, Janiya. Goddam it! *(The crying continues. Her anger played out, CIL, still on the floor, reaches for JANIYA and pulls her into her arms. JANIYA, exhausted from grief, allows herself to be held like a child.)* Baby, it's all right… It's all right… *(Both women, overwhelmed by the discharge of their taboo truths, are empty, open, and connected in their humanity.)*

Blackout

End of Play

Miss Le Gallienne Announces the New Season

A Monologue

Cast of Characters

EVA LE GALLIENNE: A young woman, 33.

Scenes

A press conference, the bare stage of the Civic Repertory
Theatre in New York City.

Time

September, 1932.

Miss Le Gallienne Announces the New Season

Lights come up on the bare stage of the Civic Repertory Theatre in New York, September 1932. There is a single chair on the stage. The founder and director of the theatre, EVA LE GALLIENE, 33, enters. She is impeccably dressed, wearing a tailored suit with stylish gauntlet gloves. Her hair is cropped and combed back. She is holding her first press conference since she closed the theatre in the spring of 1931, taking a year off to rest and rejuvenate. Her sabbatical year, however, turned out to be far from restful. EVA was nearly burned alive in a catastrophic gas explosion, and the scandal of her live-in girlfriend's divorce made headlines around the world. She is still suffering with post-traumatic syndromes, nervous about the press conference, but determined to present herself as the composed and confident, pre-fire Eva.

EVA: Welcome to the Civic Repertory Theatre! Isn't she just a marvelous old theater...? *(She turns completely around, arms wide, taking in the sight and smell of the old theater.)* The dear old Civic Rep...! *(Facing the reporters.)* It's so wonderful to be back in New York... back with all of you... I had a lovely sabbatical year, and now I am refreshed and ready to reopen the theatre... and I thought, "What better place to hold the press conference to announce the 1932 season?" And I am not just speaking to you as the producer, Eva Le Gallienne... I am speaking for *all* the actors and designers and directors at the Civic when I thank you for your generous support of our work over the last five seasons. You have been a big part of our success. And so I hope you will be as excited as we are about the shows we have lined up for opening our new season—

But first I have to ask a favor of you—and I know that you will respect this request because it is due to recent personal circumstances... Please, no pictures today. Absolutely no pictures at all... *(She listens to a question from a reporter.)* No! I'm sorry... not even "just one." No. Please put your cameras away... *(Pause.)* Please... *(She waits.)* Thank you... I knew that you would understand. Thank you. *(Pause.)* You're wonderful... *(She is interrupted.)* What? Oh, *I* am? You're too kind... *(She is interrupted again.)* What? *(Listening to a question.)* Absolutely! *(To the reporters.)* The question was, "Will we continue to produce repertory?" *Yes!* A new play every two weeks, ten shows a season... and I promise you—you have my word as producer—that we will *never* perform the same play more than four times a week. Tell your readers if they don't like the play on Thursday, they can come back on Monday and see something completely different! For the price of a movie! *(Interrupted.)* What? *(Listening.)* No. *(She shakes her head. Pause. There is another question from a different reporter.)* The fire. He asked about the fire. I have no comment to make. *(A tense pause.)* It was a year ago, and I think everyone has read quite enough about it. I understand it made headlines around the world. *(Another tense pause. Suddenly EVA smiles.)* Including reports of my death that have been greatly exaggerated. *(Relaxing, she laughs.)* Don't print that! It's Mark Twain. *(A pause as she reconsiders.)* But, actually, there is something I would like to say about the fire... *(She pauses dramatically. This is obviously a pre-rehearsed statement:)*

There is an urgent need for federal legislation that *mandates* the addition of chemicals to propane gas that will give it a distinguishing odor. Too many people are injured or killed every year, because they are unable to detect a leak or a buildup of the gas until it is too late. Your readers can let their representatives know that this regulation must be passed and passed now, before any more lives are lost.

Now... Can we *finally* get to the reason for this press conference? *(Pause.)* Ladies and gentlemen—drum roll, please!—the 1932 season at the Civic Repertory! "Something old, something new, something borrowed *and* something blue!" We're going to lead off with the "something old"—a revival of my Broadway hit, *Liliom*... ten years ago! And I am delighted to announce that we will be bringing back my former leading man and dear friend, the talented Joseph Schildkraut—*(Suddenly EVA screams, her hands flying up to her face. A photographer has set off a flashbulb. In a complete panic, EVA backs into the chair, trips, and falls to the floor. From the floor, her face still covered, she lashes out at the photographer.)*

No pictures! I said *no pictures*! What is *wrong* with you! You *don't know*... you don't *know* what that flashbulb, that... *light*, that... *sound*...does to me! I had my hands nearly *burned off* in an explosion! *(She pauses, catching her breath. Slowly she uncovers her face and lifts her head to face the audience.)* I am really quite sick... *(Long pause. She collects herself, rises slowly, and sits down, nursing her hands. Attempting to focus her thoughts, she begins again.)*

Where were we...? *(Someone has said something.)* Ah. "Something old, something new, something borrowed, something blue..." Something old. *Liliom.* With Joseph Schildkraut. He will be joining us for the entire season. *(Pause.)* Something new... *Dear Jane...* a new play about Jane Austin. Miss Hutchinson will be taking on the role of the famous author, and I will be playing her sister Cassandra... *(She pauses.)* Something borrowed—borrowed from Shakespeare. That will be a play—a verse drama—about Lady Macbeth when she was a young girl—*(She breaks off suddenly.)*

What are you staring at? *(Pause.)* You're looking at my hands, aren't you? *(A long pause. Modeling the gloves, she speaks as if giving dictation.)* "Miss Le Gallienne is wearing a pair of Chanel gauntlet gloves, from Paris... The gloves are taupe suede, with scalloped edging, featuring a fold-up option. *(A beat.)* Miss Le Gallienne is wearing the cuffs down." *(She drops her hands back in her lap and faces the reporters dispassionately.)*

"Something old, something new... something borrowed...." Yes, our third play. The verse drama... "Who was Lady Macbeth?" *That* is the question. Who was she before she became the woman whose bloody hands can never be clean again...? *(EVA stops abruptly. She studies her hands.)*

I paint my hands for the stage. With tempera. I contour them by painting in shadows and highlights. It takes a half an hour for each hand. *(She turns her hands over.)* I glue a fingernail on the second joint of this finger... *(She indicates the little finger of her right hand.)* The third joint was completely destroyed. And then I choreograph the play. *(Pause.)* I plot out every single movement—every position for each hand, for each finger, for every single minute of the play. I rehearse my hands as if they were little dancers. Ten little dancers. That is so that their disfigurement will not distract the audience from the play.

(Suddenly she looks up.) "If everybody minded their own business, the world would go around a great deal faster than it does." Do you know who said that? *(Pause.)* The Duchess. The Duchess in *Alice in Wonderland*. And *that* shall be our fourth play... "Something blue," like Alice's dress. Josephine Hutchinson will be playing Alice. Jo, of course, is the actress who has been by my side, night and day, for four years. But you knew that. I'm surprised you haven't asked me about the divorce. You all ran stories on her husband's trip to Reno last year. *(Long pause. EVA studies her hands.)*

Jo was at the top of the stairs. She was standing just above me when I struck the match... *(EVA looks up.)* Here's a riddle for you... Who said, "It's no use going back to yesterday, because

I was a different person then"? *(Pause.)* Alice says it... to the Mock Turtle.

(Someone says something.) What? *(The question is repeated.)* Why should we postpone the press conference? *(Pause.)* What? *(Pause.)* If I am having difficulty, it is because *you* keep interrupting me. But I understand why you are doing it. You are reporters. This is your job, to get the story, and it has become clear to me that the only way I am going to get through this, is to give it to you.

(Rising, EVA launches briskly into the narrative.) We were at my home in Connecticut, Josephine and I. We had just closed our fifth season, and I had announced that I would be taking a year off, to travel, to come back with new ideas... It was a beautiful day in June—warm, sunny—and I was pruning the rose bushes. Because of the thorns, I was wearing a long-sleeved flannel shirt and a thick pair of workman's overalls. This is an important detail. I was completely covered... except my hands.

I remember the caretaker was calling me. She wanted to wash her dog, but she was having difficulty getting the hot water heater to light in her cottage. I told her I would be down when I finished with the roses... which was about a half hour later. That was a half hour for the gas to build up, because she had left the valve open. She didn't realize, of course. None of us did.

Well... I finished with the roses and walked to the top of the basement stairs. I put a cigarette in my mouth. Jo was behind me. On the way down the stairs, I reached out and struck the match against the basement wall. *(Slight pause.)* There was a tremendous roar as the entire basement erupted. The air itself was on fire, everywhere... I covered my face with my hands and ran back up the stairs. Jo was ahead of me, at the top. She was burned from the heat, but she was not on fire. *I* was on fire. My hair was in flames. I ran to the sink in the kitchen to put them out... and then I saw that my clothes were burning ... and I ran out to the yard, tearing them off as I ran and rolling on the ground.

And that was when I saw my hands... *(She holds them.)* The skin was hanging off them in great bloody strips. *(Pause.)* The pain was so extreme, I felt them separate from my body. *(Brief pause.)* And then I blacked out.

(She sits.) My hands had covered my face, my eyes, my nose, my mouth. They saved my sight, they saved my lungs, they saved my looks, my life, my career. But they couldn't... they... *(She stops abruptly and looks up.)*

I came here today to share my art with you. But you want something else. You want to see my hands, don't you? Shall I take off my gloves? *(Someone has said something.)* Don't be silly. Of course, you want to see them. Everybody wants to see them. Everybody wants to see my scars... *(She pulls one of the gloves off, but cradles the hand from view.)*

What you have to understand is that they weren't hands anymore... When they unwrapped the bandages, they were just these two masses of flesh, swollen so badly, they were utterly shapeless. Not even a hint of fingers.... They had no apparent bone-structure at all. The doctor had to come every day and whittle them down... picking away at the dead tissue where the fingers were all webbed together, like a duck's foot. He asked if he could do it without the use of an anesthetic, because he needed to know where there was still nerve supply. It was excruciating. *(Pause.)* I had to sleep at night with splints on my fingers. Endless surgeries... grafting skin, reattaching ligament.

(Long pause.) I am telling you this, so that you will understand what you are looking at. *(She begins weeping.)* My hands may

appear grotesque or pathetic, but you must remember what they have been through. It is not *fair* to judge them by some standard of beauty that was left behind in the ashes of that basement! You must judge them as you would a soldier... one who sacrificed his life to save his company. You must— *(Someone is speaking from the side of the stage. EVA looks over toward the wings.)* What? *(Answering the offstage person.)* I'm announcing the season... *(She turns back to the reporters and, overwhelmed with confusion, freezes. Slowly, she puts the glove back on the naked hand. Rising with dignity, she holds up a hand in a gesture of warding off.)* Thank you. *(Turning to exit.)* No pictures... No pictures, please. *(She exits.)*

Blackout

End of Play

Acknowledgements

I want to thank Sheryl Lee Ralph for her interest in and support of *Black Star*, Julia Reddy for her support of and inspiration for *Easter Sunday*, Kathe Mull for directing the original production of *52 Pickup*, Juli Settlemire for directing *Lighting Martha*, and Brittany Parker for her interpretation *Miss Le Gallienne Announces the New Season*. I am unendingly grateful for the dramaturgical skills and friendship of Fae Spath. Of course, there are so many more... friends who were willing to read first drafts with me, discuss the problems with the plays, hold my hand through the tougher parts of the process. I'm grateful to the producers of new play festivals, the the Dramatists Guild, and to the International Centre for Women Playwrights.

Other Drama Collections by Carolyn Gage

The Second Coming of Joan of Arc and Selected Plays
Nine Short Plays
Three Comedies
Black Eye and Other Short Plays
Starting From Zero: One-Act Plays About Lesbians in Love
The Triple Goddess: Three Plays
The Very Short Plays
Monologues and Scenes for Lesbian Actors
More Monologues and Scenes for Lesbian Actors

www.ingramcontent.com/pod-product-compliance
Lightning Source LLC
Chambersburg PA
CBHW051443250726
48655CB00001B/206

9 781794 767577